福建的文化与自然遗产

CULTURAL
AND
NATURAL
HERITAGE
IN FUJIAN

福建省人民政府新闻办公室 编

海峡出版发行集团
THE STRAITS PUBLISHING & DISTRIBUTING GROUP
福建人民出版社

《福建的文化与自然遗产》编委会

目　录

001 **武夷山**

002 遗产价值
004 武夷山览胜

006 举世罕见的物种基因库——武夷山国家级自然保护区
010 武夷山水的灵秀之源——九曲溪生态保护区
014 钟灵毓秀，茶即山水的大美之地——武夷山国家风景名胜区
022 沉睡千年的古国文明——古汉城遗址

025 **福建土楼**

028 遗产价值
030 福建土楼探秘

032 永定初溪土楼群
034 永定洪坑土楼群
037 永定高北土楼群
039 永定南溪土楼沟景区
042 南靖田螺坑土楼群
046 南靖河坑土楼群
048 南靖云水谣景区
051 华安大地土楼群

053 **泰宁丹霞**

054 遗产价值
058 泰宁丹霞问奇

060 丹霞崖壁
061 丹霞方山
062 石峰石柱
064 丹霞石墙
065 崩积堆和崩积巨石
066 丹霞沟谷
068 丹霞洞穴
070 丹霞穿洞
071 天穹岩
072 自然之歌

077　**鼓浪屿：历史国际社区**

078　遗产价值
081　鼓浪撷英

081　天风海涛——自然景观与文化遗迹
083　文化交融——公共地界与国际社区
088　万国建筑——一席流动的盛宴
094　外来宗教——左手医疗，右手教育
097　音乐体育——永不止息的回响

099　**泉州：宋元中国的世界海洋商贸中心**

100　遗产价值
103　千年商港回望

104　招商入番 祈风祭海
110　物华天宝 誉满十洲
113　梯航万国 无远不至
120　海滨邹鲁 光明之城

129　**三坊七巷**

130　遗产价值
136　三坊七巷漫步

140　林觉民故居
141　水榭戏台
142　欧阳氏民居
143　陈承裘故居
144　严复故居
145　二梅书屋
146　小黄楼
147　林氏民居
148　沈葆桢故居

149　**海上丝绸之路（中国福建段）**

150　遗产价值
152　海上丝路寻迹

156　闽中隆兴
160　东方第一大港风采
166　郑和七下西洋
171　漳州月港崛起

173　闽浙木拱廊桥（福建部分）
—

174　遗产价值
178　木拱廊桥探幽

182　万安桥
184　千乘桥
186　杨梅州桥
188　鸾峰桥
189　大宝桥
190　广利桥和广福桥
192　赤溪桥
193　后山桥
194　洋后桥

195　闽南红砖建筑
—

196　遗产价值
198　红砖古厝寻踪

198　蔡氏古民居
210　大嶝郑氏聚落

219　万里茶道（中国福建段）
—

220　遗产价值
228　茶道起点访古

228　武夷茶产区
232　九曲溪茶事题刻
234　下梅传统村落
236　闽赣古驿道及分水关遗址

CONTENTS

001 Mount Wuyi

003 Universal Value

005 Tours around Mount Wuyi

007 A Rare Species Gene Pool: Wuyishan National Nature Reserve

010 The Source of Mount Wuyi's Natural Charm: Nine-Bend Stream Ecological Protection Area

015 A Grand Beauty Endowed with the Most Talented Man and the Best Tea: Wuyishan National Scenic Area

023 The Ancient Civilization in Its Millenary Slumber: Remains of the Ancient Han Dynasty

025 Fujian Tulou

028 Universal Value

031 Getting into Fujian Tulou

032 Chuxi Tulou Cluster in Yongding

035 Hongkeng Tulou Cluster in Yongding

037 Gaobei Tulou Cluster in Yongding

039 Nanxi Tulougou Scenic Area in Yongding

042 Tianluokeng Tulou Cluster in Nanjing

047 Hekeng Tulou Cluster in Nanjing

048 Yunshuiyao Scenic Area in Nanjing

051 Dadi Tulou Cluster in Hua'an

053 Taining Danxia

055 Universal Value

059 Exploring Taining Danxia

060 Danxia Cliffs

061 Danxia Mesas

062 Danxia Peaks and Pillars

064 Danxia Stone Walls

065 Colluvia and Colluvial Giant Stones

066 Danxia Valleys

068 Danxia Caves

070 Danxia Arches

071 The Sky-Dome Rock

073 The Songs of Nature

077 **Kulangsu: a Historic International Settlement**
—

079 **Universal Value**
082 **The Beauty of Kulangsu**

082 Paradise on Earth: A Collection of Natural and Cultural Wonders
084 Cultural Integration: Public Land and International Settlement
089 Rich Diversity of Architectural Styles: A Feast for the Eye
094 Foreign Religions: Spreading the Gospel Through Medicine and Education
098 Ongoing Glory: Island of Music and Sports

099 **Quanzhou: Emporium of the World in Song-Yuan China**
—

100 **Universal Value**
103 **A Look back at the Millenary Port of Quanzhou**

104 Attracting Merchants to Quanzhou's Shores and Worshipping the Wind and Sea Gods
110 Land of Abundant Treasure and Wealth
113 The Path to Foreign Countries
121 Land of Culture and Education & City of Light

129 **Three Lanes and Seven Alleys**
—

131 **Universal Value**
137 **A Stroll around Three Lanes and Seven Alleys**

140 Lin Juemin's Former Residence
141 The Waterside Theatre
142 Ouyang Family Residence
143 Chen Chengqiu's Former Residence
144 Yan Fu's Former Residence
145 Ermei Study
146 Xiaohuanglou
147 Lin Family Residence
148 Shen Baozhen's Former Residence

149 **The Maritime Silk Road (Fujian Section in China)**
—

151 **Universal Value**

152 **Development of the Maritime Silk Road**

156 The Pride of Fujian

160 The Largest Port in the East

167 Zheng He's Seven Voyages to the West

172 The Rise of Zhangzhou Yuegang Port

173 **Wooden Arch Lounge Bridges in Fujian and Zhejiang Provinces (Fujian Section)**
—

174 **Universal Value**

179 **The Charming Wooden Arch Lounge Bridges**

182 Wan'an Bridge

184 Qiansheng Bridge

186 Yangmeizhou Bridge

188 Luanfeng Bridge

189 Dabao Bridge

190 Guangli Bridge and Guangfu Bridge

192 Chixi Bridge

193 Houshan Bridge

194 Yanghou Bridge

195 **The Red Brick Buildings of Southern Fujian**
—

197 **Universal Value**

199 **Visiting the Ancient Red Brick Houses**

199 Cai Family Residence

211 Zheng Family Residence in Dadeng Town

219 **The Ten-Thousand-*Li* Tea Road (Fujian Section in China)**
—

221 **Universal Value**

229 **Remains at the Starting Point of the Tea Road**

229 Tea Planting and Processing Area in Mount Wuyi

233 The Cliff Inscriptions about Tea Affairs along Nine-Bend Stream

235 The Traditional Xiamei Village

237 The Fujian-Jiangxi Ancient Roads and Fenshuiguan Historic Site

武夷山
Mount Wuyi

碧水丹山——武夷山。（郑友裕 摄）
The jade water and red mountains in Mount Wuyi. (Photo by Zheng Youyu)

遗产价值

　　武夷山脉是中国东南部最负盛名的生物多样性保护区，也是大量古代孑遗物种的避难所，其中许多生物为中国所特有。九曲溪两岸峡谷秀美，寺院庙宇众多，虽然其中不少早已成为废墟，但曾为理学的发展和传播提供了良好的环境。自 11 世纪以来，理学对东亚地区的文化产生了相当深刻的影响。公元前 2 世纪时，汉朝统治者在武夷山附近的城村建立了一处较大的行政首府，厚重坚实的围墙环绕四周，极具考古价值。

　　武夷山作为世界文化与自然遗产，于 1999 年 12 月被正式列入《世界遗产名录》。

◎ 武夷仙境。（晏音 摄）
A fairyland—Mount Wuyi. (Photo by Yan Yin)

Universal Value

Mount Wuyi is the most outstanding area for biodiversity conservation in southeast China and a refuge for a large number of ancient, relict species, many of them endemic to China. The serene beauty of the dramatic gorges of Nine-Bend Stream, with its numerous temples and monasteries, many now in ruins, provided the setting for development and spread of Neo-Confucianism, which has been influential in the cultures of East Asia since the 11th century. In the 2nd century BCE, a large administrative capital was built at nearby Chengcun by the Han Dynasty rulers. Its massive walls enclose an archaeological site of great significance.

Mount Wuyi was inscribed on the World Heritage List as a world cultural and natural property in December 1999.

武夷山览胜

　　武夷山世界文化与自然遗产包含四个区域：位于西部的武夷山国家级自然保护区、位于中部的九曲溪生态保护区、位于东部的武夷山国家风景名胜区和独矗于东南方向15千米以外的古汉城遗址保护区。武夷山世界文化与自然遗产总占地面积为1,070.44平方千米，被占地面积为401.7平方千米的缓冲地带环绕，因其文化、风光及生物多样性价值而被联合国教科文组织纳入《世界遗产名录》。

◎ 武夷山自然保护区断裂带。（郑友裕 摄）
The fault zone at Wuyishan National Nature Reserve. (Photo by Zheng Youyu)

◎ 古汉城遗址。（郑友裕 摄）

Remains of the Ancient Han Dynasty. (Photo by Zheng Youyu)

Tours around Mount Wuyi

The property consists of four protected areas: Wuyishan National Nature Reserve in the west, Nine-Bend Stream Ecological Protection Area in the centre and Wuyishan National Scenic Area in the east, the three of which are contiguous, while the Protection Area for Remains of the Ancient Han Dynasty is a separate area, about 15km to the southeast. Totalling 107,044 hectare, the property is surrounded by a buffer zone of 40,170 hectare and has been inscribed for cultural as well as scenic and biodiversity values.

■ 举世罕见的物种基因库——武夷山国家级自然保护区

武夷山国家级自然保护区位于武夷山、建阳、光泽三个县市的结合部，西北部与江西省铅山县比邻。由于地壳运动，抬升、褶皱、断裂、剥蚀等地质活动曾经在此处频繁发生，从而形成高山、峡谷、孤峰和绝壁等特殊地貌，造就了今日山雄、谷狭、滩险、水秀、季相分明、奇花遍野、芳草铺地、古木参天的优良环境。这里禽兽徜徉、虫鱼自由，是植物的圣地、动物的乐园。其中挂墩、大竹岚、三港等地是享誉世界的生物圣地，有着"昆虫世界""蛇的王国""鸟的乐园""研究亚洲两栖爬行动物的钥匙"等美称，是世界所公认的生物之窗。

◎ 生物圣地大竹岚。（郑友裕 摄）
Dazhulan, a renowned heaven for wildlife. (Photo by Zheng Youyu)

A Rare Species Gene Pool: Wuyishan National Nature Reserve

Wuyishan National Nature Reserve is located at the junction of Wuyishan City, Jianyang County and Guangze County. Northwest it is adjacent to Yanshan County in Jiangxi Prvince. As a result of crustal movement, erosion and other geological activities which formed high mountains, narrow valleys, solitary peaks and cliffs and other unique landforms, thereby creating today's wonderful environment here of mountains, vales, shoals, waters, distinct seasons, different kinds of flowers, green grass spreading over the ground, towering ancient trees, etc., it is also a special paradise for plants and animals. Guadun, Dazhulan, San'gang and some other places here provide a world-renowned heaven for wildlife, with the reputation of "insect world", "snake kingdom", "bird paradise", "key to studying Asian amphibians and reptiles", etc., which is recognized as the window into the world's natural life.

◎ 武夷山珍稀禽类——白鹇。（郑友裕 摄）
A rare bird in Mount Wuyi—the silver pheasant. (Photo by Zheng Youyu)

◎ 武夷山珍稀禽类——黄腹角雉。（郑友裕 摄）
A rare bird in Mount Wuyi—the yellow-bellied tragopan. (Photo by Zheng Youyu)

◎ 武夷山珍稀动物——短尾猴。（郑友裕 摄）
Rare animals in Mount Wuyi—macaque monkeys. (Photo by Zheng Youyu)

　　自 19 世纪下半叶法国传教士在这里收集到许多动植物新种之后，
武夷山引起了西方生物学界的广泛关注。此后曾有众多的外国博物学者
到这里进行生物学考察和收集。世界上许多著名的自然博物馆，如法国
国家自然历史博物馆、英国自然历史博物馆、德国柏林自然历史博物馆、
美国自然历史博物馆、美国国立博物馆和中国上海自然博物馆都有大批
出自武夷山的动物标本，其中有数百种成为模式标本。20 世纪前期分别
由英国和美国出版的《中国东部的鸟类手册》及《中国的爬行动物》等
有影响的著作，都与这一地区有着密切的渊源关系。

Ever since French missionaries collected many new species of plants and animals here in the second half of the 19th century, Mount Wuyi had attracted extensive attention from Western biological circles. Since then, a large number of foreign naturalists had come here for biological investigation and collection. Many famous natural museums in the world, such as those in Paris, London, Berlin, New York, Washington and Shanghai, have a large number of animal specimens from Mount Wuyi, among which hundreds became type specimens. Some influential works such as *A Handbook of the Birds of Eastern China* and *The Reptiles of China* respectively published in Britain and the United States in the early 20th century were also closely related to this region.

◎ 武夷山国家级自然保护区的南方铁杉林。（郑友裕 摄）
A tsuga chinensis forest in Wuyishan National Nature Reserve. (Photo by Zheng Youyu)

■ 武夷山水的灵秀之源——九曲溪生态保护区

　　九曲溪是发源于武夷山脉主峰——黄岗山西南麓的溪流，澄澈清莹，经星村镇由西向东穿过武夷山国家风景名胜区，盈盈一水，折为九曲，因此得名。九曲溪上游为生态保护区，这里高峰林立，峡谷纵横，网状的溪涧流量充沛，奇泉飞瀑遍布，珍禽异兽结队，大片的原始森林中有数千株古树名木。

■ The Source of Mount Wuyi's Natural Charm: Nine-Bend Stream Ecological Protection Area

Nine-Bend Stream originates from the main peak of Mount Wuyi—at the southwest slope of Huanggang Mountain; its clear waters drift through ancient Xingcun Township, flowing from west to east through Wuyishan National Scenic Area around nine bends, hence the name. The upstream area of Nine-Bend Steam is an ecological reserve. The well-watered ravines intertwine with dense peaks, which shapes the spectacular scenery of mountains and streams. It is a paradise for rare animals and birds. And there are thousands of precious ancient trees in the virgin forests here.

◎ 九曲溪发源地——黄岗山。（郑友裕 摄）
Huanggang Mountain, the source of Nine-Bend Stream. (Photo by Zheng Youyu)

◎ 九曲溪生态保护区内的奇泉飞瀑。（郑友裕 摄）
Lovely creeks and spectacular waterfalls in Nine-Bend Stream Ecological Protection Area. (Photo by Zheng Youyu)

◎ 天游峰峰顶俯瞰九曲。（郑友裕 摄）
Overlooking Nine-Bend Stream from Tianyou Peak. (Photo by Zheng Youyu)

　　九曲溪下游东部的壮观地貌成就了其非凡景色，这里已进入武夷山国家风景名胜区，红色砂岩构成的巨石绝壁陡然而立，形成长达 10 千米的天际线。它们以 200—400 米之高度耸峙于河床之上，底部深藏于清澈幽深的河水之中。这些古老崖壁上的山径不可错过，沿其登临峰顶，游客便可以鸟瞰九曲风光。

As part of Wuyishan National Scenic Area, the spectacular landforms in the eastern part of Nine-Bend Stream's downstream are of exceptional scenic quality, with isolated, sheer-sided monoliths of the local red sandstone. They dominate the skyline for a tortuous 10km section of the river, standing 200—400 meters above the riverbed, and terminate in clear, deep water. The ancient cliff tracks are an important dimension of the site, allowing the visitors to get a bird's-eye view of the river from the summit.

■ 钟灵毓秀、茶即山水的大美之地——武夷山国家风景名胜区

　　武夷山是一处被保护了超过 1,200 年的美丽景观。其风景名胜区所包含的九曲溪下游沿岸庙宇众多，虽然多数已成废墟，但曾为自 11 世纪以来在东亚地区影响深远的政治哲学思想——理学的发展与传播提供了良好的环境。此外，这里还可以看到墓葬、题刻和藏着历史可以追溯至商代的木质船棺的岩穴，以及多座道教寺观遗迹。

◎ 六曲有 23 处摩崖石刻。（郑友裕 摄）
There are 23 stone inscriptions at the sixth bend. (Photo by Zheng Youyu)

Remains of boat-shaped coffins in a rock cave at the fourth bend. (Photo by Zheng Youyu)

■ A Grand Beauty Endowed with the Most Talented Man and the Best Tea: Wuyishan National Scenic Area

Mount Wuyi is a landscape of great beauty that has been protected for more than twelve centuries. Along the downstream of Nine-Bend Stream in the scenic area are numerous temples and monasteries, many now in ruins, which provided the setting for the development and spread of Neo-Confucianism, a political philosophy which has been very influential in the cultures of East Asia since the 11th century. In addition, the area boasts tombs, inscriptions and rock shelters with wooden boat-shaped coffins dating back to the Shang Dynasty (over 3,000 years ago), and the remains of many Taoist temples and monasteries.

理学之集大成者朱熹（1130—1200）与武夷山有着十分密切的关系，山中也留下了许多与他相关的遗迹。据文献记载，武夷山朱熹讲学处有武夷精舍、冲佑观、水帘洞、金谷洞四处，朱熹手书的石刻有十余处。武夷精舍故址位于五曲溪畔隐屏峰下的平林渡。精舍由朱熹于宋淳熙十年（1183）亲自擘画、营建，被现代海内外学者喻为"中国第一所私立大学"。朱熹在此广收门徒，倡道讲学，著书立说。书院开办期间，理学学术活动活跃，朱熹的思想体系也逐步走向成熟。

Zhu Xi (1130—1200), the one who most epitomized Neo-Confucianism, had a such close relationship with Mount Wuyi that there are many historical mementos related to him in here. According to the records, Zhu Xi gave lectures in several places in Mount Wuyi, including Wuyi Academy, Chongyou Taoist Temple, Water Curtain Cave and Jingu Cave, and there were more than 10 stone inscriptions of Zhu Xi's calligraphy. Wuyi Academy Site is located at Pinglin Ferry at the foot of Yinping Peak by the fifth bend. The academy was designed and built by Zhu Xi in 1183, and modern scholars at home and abroad call it "the first private university in China". Zhu Xi gathered disciples here, taught and wrote books. Ever since the opening of Wuyi Academy, academic activities of Neo-Confucianism were active here, and Zhu Xi's ideological system gradually matured.

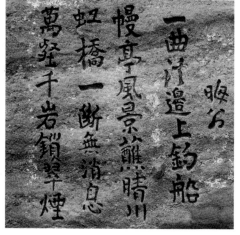

◎ 朱熹手书石刻。（郑友裕 摄）

Stone inscriptions of Zhu Xi's calligraphy. (Photo by Zheng Youyu)

◎ 武夷精舍故址。（郑友裕 摄）
Wuyi Academy Site. (Photo by Zheng Youyu)

◎ 大红袍母树。（郑友裕 摄）
The Mother Trees of Dahongpao. (Photo by Zheng Youyu)

　　武夷山不独以山水之奇而奇，更以茶产之奇而奇，其碧水丹山的独特自然环境所孕育的武夷岩茶有着"岩骨花香"的优秀品质。武夷山风景名胜区自古以来就是武夷岩茶的重要产地，沿着岩骨花香漫游道行走，可经过部分核心产区，终点处可见驰名中外的大红袍母树。300 多岁的古茶树不仅显示着时光的印记，还承载着"大红袍外交"这样的过往辉煌。

Mount Wuyi is not only unique in its landscape, but also unmatched by its famous tea. The unique natural environment of jade waters and red mountains breeds Wuyi Rock Tea, which has the excellent quality of "rock bone and flower fragrance". Since ancient times, the scenic area of Mount Wuyi has been the core tea producing area of Wuyi Rock Tea, part of which can be reached by walking along the Rock Bone and Flower Fragrance Wandering Path. You can see the world-famous 300-year-old Mother Trees of Dahongpao at the end of this path, which not only show the passage of time, but also bear the glory of "Dahongpao diplomacy".

◎ 岩骨花香漫游道。（郑友裕 摄）
Rock Bone and Flower Fragrance Wandering Path. (Photo by Zheng Youyu)

◎ 位于溪南的一线天。（郑友裕 摄）

A Sliver of Sky at South of the Stream. (Photo by Zheng Youyu)

武夷山的名胜古迹多集中在九曲溪一带，但溪南也有绝景，令人流连忘返，山北亦有胜境，可探丛林苍翠。如果把溪南和山北看作武夷山国家风景名胜区的南北极，这溪南绝景与山北胜境的"两极"风光绝对值得一看。

Most of the scenic spots and historic sites of Mount Wuyi are concentrated in the Nine-Bend Stream area, but there is also spectacular scenery to the south of the stream, which is so enticing that it makes people linger there and forget to return. Additionally, there are scenic spots to the north of the mountains, where one can even explore a verdant jungle. Therefore, South of the Stream and North of the Mountains are regarded as the south and north poles of Wuyishan National Scenic Area, both of which are definitely worth a visit.

◎ 巧妙地建于岩隙之中的妙莲寺，位于山北莲花峰。（郑友裕 摄）

Miaolian Temple at Lianhua Peak, North of the Mountains, ingeniously built into the rock gaps. (Photo by Zheng Youyu)

■ 沉睡千年的古国文明——古汉城遗址

　　闽越王城遗址坐落在武夷山市兴田镇城村，是中国长江以南保存比较完整的一座汉代古城址。它在选址、建筑手法和风格上独具特色，为当时全国地方诸侯国都邑的代表和典范，体现了业已消逝的闽越古国文明。闽越国是福建历史上地方割据政权中存在时间最长、也最为强盛的诸侯国。闽越王无诸称得上是"开闽始祖"——他立国称王，建立闽越国，揭开了福建文明史的第一页。

◎ 闽越王像。（郑友裕 摄）
The statue of King Minyue. (Photo by Zheng Youyu)

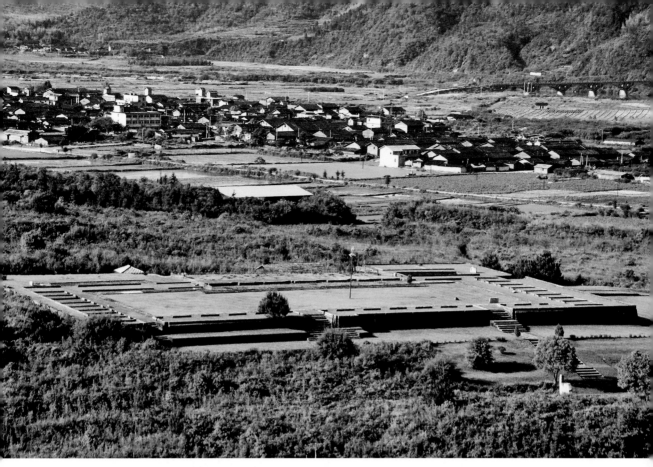

◎ 遗址上 2,000 多米长的夯土城墙轮廓依稀可辨。（文脉 供图）

The outline of the earth-rammed city wall of more than 2,000 meters long at the site is still distinguishable. (Courtesy of Wenmai)

■ The Ancient Civilization in Its Millenary Slumber: Remains of the Ancient Han Dynasty

Minyue Kingdom Site is located in Chengcun Village, Xingtian Township, Wuyishan City. It is an ancient Han Dynasty city site in relatively good preservation state compared with other ancient Chinese cities unearthed to the south of the Yangtze River. Being unique in site selection, architectural techniques and styles, it was representative of the national capitals of various vassal states at that time, embodying the vanished ancient civilization of Minyue. Minyue was the most powerful vassal state in the history of Fujian Province and existed for the longest time. The founder, Wuzhu, is called "the ancestor of Fujian" because he proclaimed himself king and established the State of Minyue, opening the first page of the history of Fujian civilization.

遗址自 1958 年试掘以来，陆续出土了数万件汉代文物，具有很高的价值，其中有许多在全国同类文物中位居前列。遗址上还有御井一口，至今仍然水质纯净，清冽可饮，被称为"华夏第一古井"。

Since the site was tentatively excavated in 1958, thousands of Han Dynasty cultural relics of high value have been unearthed successively, many of which are in the forefront compared to similar cultural relics in the country. There is a royal well at the site known as "the first ancient well of China", in which the water is still pure, cool and drinkable.

◎ 王城御井。（郑友裕 摄）
The royal well. (Photo by Zheng Youyu)

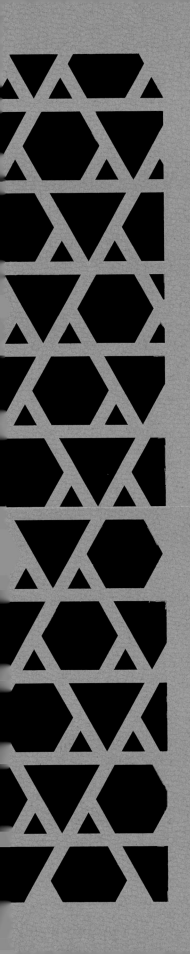

遗产价值

　　列入《世界遗产名录》的福建土楼包括建于 15 世纪至 20 世纪的 46 栋建筑物，位于福建省西南部，主要分布于龙岩市永定区和漳州市南靖县、华安县。土楼是坐落在稻田、茶山和烟草地间的土制房子，大多有几层楼高，沿着一个向内、呈圆形或方形的楼层平面建造，每座建筑可容纳多达 800 人居住。这些建筑是为了防卫而建造，环绕着一个中央露天庭院，只有一个入口，一楼以上才有窗户，可观外面的世界。一座土楼往往就是一个家族的聚居地，是村里的构成单位，被称为"家庭小王国"或"繁华的小城市"。土楼以高大的泥墙为特色，墙面由瓦屋顶覆盖，宽屋檐悬挑。

　　最精巧的土楼建筑可追溯到 17 和 18 世纪。建筑物里，不同家庭采用垂直划分区域而居住，平均使用每个楼层，每层有两个或三个房间供每个家庭使用。与它们朴素的外表相比，土楼内部的设计则表现得相当舒适，而且常常装饰精美。土楼被作为建筑传统和功能的独特代表列为世界遗产，它们体现了特殊的社区生活和防御性功能，与环境和谐共存，是人类住所的杰出范例。

　　福建土楼作为文化遗产，于 2008 年 7 月被正式列入《世界遗产名录》。

Universal Value

Fujian Tulou is a property of 46 buildings constructed between the 15th and 20th centuries in the southwest of Fujian Province, mainly located in Yongding District of Longyan, and Nanjing County and Hua'an County in Zhangzhou. Set amongst rice, tea and tobacco fields, the Tulou are earthen houses. Several storeys high, they were built along an inward-looking, circular or square floor plane as housing for up to 800 people each. They were built for defence purposes around a central open courtyard with only one entrance and windows to the outside only above the first floor. Housing a whole clan, the houses functioned as village units and were known as "a little kingdom for the family" or "small bustling city". They feature tall fortified mud walls capped by tiled roofs with wide over-hanging eaves.

◎ 洪坑土楼群振成楼内的精美内饰。（王福平 摄）

The exquisite interior of Zhenchenglou in Hongkeng Tulou Cluster. (Photo by Wang Fuping)

The most elaborate structures date back to the 17th and 18th centuries. The buildings were divided vertically between families with each disposing of two or three rooms on each floor. In contrast with their plain exterior, the inside of the Tulou were built for comfort and were often highly decorated. They are inscribed as exceptional examples of a building tradition and function exemplifying a particular type of communal living and defensive organization, and, in terms of their harmonious relationship with their environment, an outstanding example of human settlement.

Fujian Tulou was inscribed on the World Heritage List as a cultural property in July 2008.

福建土楼探秘

　　福建土楼数以万计，或"成群结队"，形成土楼村、土楼沟、土楼"长城"；或"孤傲独居"，散落在闽西南崇山峻岭之中。成千上万座土楼，因地形、条件或风水所限，形成了除方楼、圆楼、五凤楼以外的多边形楼，包括五角楼、六角楼、八角楼、"日"字形楼、"吕"字形楼、"富"字形楼等等，显得那样千姿百态、丰富多彩。

　　2008 年 7 月，福建土楼中有 46 座土楼被正式列入《世界遗产名录》，其中包括龙岩市永定区"三群两楼"（指初溪土楼群、洪坑土楼群、高北土楼群和振福楼、衍香楼），漳州市南靖县"两群两楼"（指田螺坑土楼群、河坑土楼群与和贵楼、怀远楼）以及漳州市华安县的大地土楼群。

◎ 初溪土楼群集庆楼的内景。（王福平 摄）
The interior of Jiqinglou in Chuxi Tulou Cluster. (Photo by Wang Fuping)

◎ 高北土楼群美丽如画的承启楼和世泽楼。（胡家新 摄）

The picturesque Chengqilou and Shizelou in Gaobei Tulou Cluster. (Photo by Hu Jiaxin)

Getting into Fujian Tulou

There are tens of thousands of Tulou scattered in the mountains of southwestern Fujian. Their shapes have been influenced by terrain, Feng Shui and weather conditions. As a result, there are many more polygonal shaped buildings in addition to the square, circular and pagoda like ones mentioned here today.

In July 2008, forty-six of the numerous Fujian Tulou buildings were officially inscribed on the UNESCO World Heritage List. From Yongding District of Longyan, there is Chuxi Tulou Cluster, Hongkeng Tulou Cluster, Gaobei Tulou Cluster, Zhenfulou and Yanxianglou. From Nanjing County of Zhangzhou, there is Tianluokeng Tulou Cluster, Hekeng Tulou Cluster, Heguilou and Huaiyuanlou. Finally, in Hua'an County, Zhangzhou, the Dadi Tulou Cluster.

◎ "三圆一方"由左向右依次为余庆楼、庚庆楼、集庆楼、绳庆楼。（王福平 摄）

Left to right: Yuqinglou, Gengqinglou, Jiqinglou and Shengqinglou (the square one). (Photo by Wang Fuping)

■ 永定初溪土楼群

初溪土楼群位于龙岩市永定区下洋镇初溪村，规模宏大，类型丰富，有长方形、正方形、圆形、椭圆形、八角形等多种外形，显得生动而立体。其中被列入《世界遗产名录》的土楼就有集庆楼、庚庆楼、余庆楼、绳庆楼、善庆楼、锡庆楼、共庆楼、福庆楼、华庆楼、藩庆楼共 10 座土楼。它们大多保存完好，至今还保留着原有的建筑格局，具有较高的历史价值、建筑学价值和艺术价值。

■ Chuxi Tulou Cluster in Yongding

Chuxi Tulou Cluster is located in Chuxi Village, Xiayang Town, in Yongding District of Longyan. Comparatively large and vast in designs, Chuxi Tulou Cluster consists of rectangular, square, elliptical, and octagonal shaped buildings. Among these structures are Jiqinglou, Gengqinglou, Yuqinglou, Shengqinglou, Shanqinglou, Xiqinglou, Gongqinglou, Fuqinglou, Huaqinglou and Fanqinglou. These are ten out of the forty-six Tulou listed as World Cultural Heritage sites. Most of them are well preserved, and still retain the original architectural structure making them rich in historical, architectural and artistic value.

© 初溪土楼群全景。（王福平摄）
Full view of Chuxi Tulou Cluster. (Photo by Wang Fuping)

■ 永定洪坑土楼群

　　洪坑土楼群位于永定区东南面的湖坑镇洪坑村，由林氏祖先始建于13世纪，保存完好的有数十座16世纪以来修建的土楼，大小交错，形态各异，主要有正方形、长方形、圆形、五凤楼、半月形及其变异形式的土楼造型。其中7座被列入《世界遗产名录》，包括振成楼、庆成楼、福裕楼、福兴楼、如升楼、光裕楼和奎聚楼。

◎ "土楼王子"振成楼。（王福平 摄）
Zhenchenglou, the "Tulou Prince". (Photo by Wang Fuping)

Hongkeng Tulou Cluster in Yongding

Hongkeng Tulou Cluster is located in Hongkeng Village of Hukeng Town which is in the southeastern part of Yongding District. The cluster was started in the 13th century by the Lin's ancestors, leaving dozens of Tulou well-preserved which had been built since the 16th century of the Ming Dynasty. The cluster mainly consists of square, rectangular and circular Tulou, half-moon shape and five-phoenix-style (pavilion) buildings. There are seven Tulou of the cluster listed as the World Heritage sites.

◎ 建于 1880 年的福裕楼，占地面积约 4,000 平方米，是土楼的杰出代表、五凤楼的经典。（赖永生 摄）
Fuyulou, built in 1880 and covering an area of about 4,000 square metres, is a five-phoenix-style building and a classic representation of its kind. (Photo by Lai Yongsheng)

◎ 如升楼占地面积约为500平方米，直径23米。楼内空间极小，仅有几户人家，是福建世遗土楼中最小的土楼。（王福平 摄）

Rushenglou, covering an area of about 500 square metres with the diameter of only 23 metres, is the smallest "pocket Tulou" out of the listed World Heritage sites. (Photo by Wang Fuping)

■ 永定高北土楼群

高北土楼群位于永定区高头乡高北村，在数十座规模不等、造型各异的土楼中，承启楼、世泽楼、五云楼、侨福楼四座土楼被列入《世界遗产名录》。承启楼为四环圆形土楼，占地面积 5,300 多平方米。它具有高大厚重、粗犷雄伟的建筑风格，悠久的历史以及独特的造型，堪称永定土楼中规模最大、环数最多的圆形土楼，享有"土楼王"的美誉。1986 年，承启楼作为"福建民居"的图案印在我国发行的中国民居邮票中。

■ Gaobei Tulou Cluster in Yongding

Gaobei Tulou Cluster is located in Gaobei Village, Gaotou Township of Yongding District. Among the many various shaped Tulou, four buildings are inscribed on the World Heritage List: Chengqilou, Shizelou, Wuyunlou and Qiaofulou. Chengqilou is a four-ring round Tulou, covering an area of more than 5,300 square metres. It is tall, heavy, rugged and majestic in style with a long history and unique shape to make it the largest Tulou out of all the Yongding Tulou. This has earned it the status and reputation as the "Tulou King". It can be found on national stamps issued in China in 1986.

◎ 世泽楼金秋晒柿。（胡家新 摄）
Drying persimmons in autumn at Shizelou. (Photo by Hu Jiaxin)

◎ "土楼王" 承启楼内景。（胡家新 摄）
The interiors of Chengqilou, praised as the "Tulou King". (Photo by Hu Jiaxin)

■ 永定南溪土楼沟景区

　　永定区南溪土楼沟景区由数百座大小不一、形态各异的土楼组成。这些土楼依山就势、错落有致地分布在南溪河两岸，延绵十几千米，形成了一处蔚为壮观的"土楼长城"。其中列入《世界遗产名录》的有振福楼和衍香楼。

■ Nanxi Tulougou Scenic Area in Yongding

The hundreds of Tulou situated in Nanxi of Yongding District are of various sizes and shapes. These earth buildings are located on either bank of the Nanxi River, stretching for more than ten kilometres and forming the spectacular "Great Wall of Tulou". Out of the cluster, Zhenfulou and Yanxianglou were listed as World Cultural Heritage sites.

◎ 数百座土楼组成的"土楼长城"奇观。（王福平 摄）
Hundreds of Tulou form the spectacular "Great Wall of Tulou". (Photo by Wang Fuping)

◎ 戏水振福楼前。（赖永生 摄）

Playing in the creek in front of Zhenfulou. (Photo by Lai Yongsheng)

振福楼建于 1913 年，占地面积 4,000 多平方米，共有 3 个厅堂，96 个房间。楼内有很多精美的装饰，琉璃瓦面，雕梁画栋，石质门框镌刻对联，门两边为砖雕花格窗棂。因其拥有高贵典雅的气质，振福楼又被称为"土楼公主"。

Built in 1913, Zhenfulou covers an area of more than 4,000 square metres, with three halls and 96 rooms. The inner ring has many beautiful decorations. The front door of the inner ring has a painted and carved beam, a glazed tile surface, and an engraved door frame. Because of its elegance, it is also known as the "Tulou Princess".

衍香楼建于 1842 年，高 3 层，占地面积约 4,300 平方米，外环为圆楼，里面一座方形院落，外圆内方，圆中有方，是福建土楼中风格较为独特的土楼。衍香楼的内厅为仿府第式建筑，雕梁画栋、古朴典雅，梁柱间"群龙腾云""卧狮踞梁"等木雕栩栩如生，墙壁上书画精美、龙飞凤舞，枋额斗拱有"五福临门"、花鸟虫鱼等艳丽多姿的彩绘。

Built in 1842, Yanxianglou has three storeys and covers an area of about 4,300 square metres. It is made up of an outer ring and a square courtyard, a unique combination. The inner hall of Yanxianglou has carved beams and elegant paintings. The wooden carvings featured inside seem to be alive while the paintings on the walls depict dancing dragons and phoenixes, flowers, birds and insects—a swirl of brilliant colours. These exquisite art on the walls brings alive poems written by past generations.

◎ 浪漫衍香楼。（赖永生 摄）
Romantic Yanxianglou. (Photo by Lai Yongsheng)

■ 南靖田螺坑土楼群

　　从龙岩市永定区高北土楼群到漳州市南靖县田螺坑土楼群大约 20 千米。列入《世界遗产名录》的田螺坑土楼群由五座保存完好的土楼组成，分别为方形的步云楼，圆形的振昌楼、瑞云楼、和昌楼和椭圆形的文昌楼。五座土楼坐落在海拔 787.8 米的湖崇山半山坡上，三面环山，前面是美丽的梯田。四座圆形土楼依山势起伏，高低错落，疏密有致，远远看去，就像装着菜的四个圆盘子，而方楼步云楼位于四座圆形土楼中间，构成一幅具有强烈视觉冲击力的美妙景观，因此被誉为"四菜一汤"，名扬天下。

■ Tianluokeng Tulou Cluster in Nanjing

There is about 20 kilometres between Yongding Gaobei Tulou Cluster in Longyan and Tianluokeng Tulou Cluster of Nanjing, Zhangzhou. The latter consists of five well-preserved Tulou, namely the square Buyunlou, the circular Zhenchanglou, Ruiyunlou, Hechanglou and the oval Wenchanglou. These Tulou are located on the slope of Hudong Mountain at an altitude of 787.8 metres and are surrounded by mountains on three sides. The square Buyunlou sits in the middle of the four circular Tulou. Some say that this looks like a Chinese dinner table with four round dishes of food and one square bowl of soup in the middle.

◎ 土楼群俯视图。（章庆煌 摄）
　　An aerial view of the Tulou cluster. (Photo by Zhang Qinghuang)

© 田螺坑土楼群仰视图。（严孙锦 摄）

An upward view of Tianluokeng Tulou Cluster. (Photo by Yan Sunjin)

■ 南靖河坑土楼群

　　河坑土楼群位于漳州市南靖县书洋镇曲江村河坑自然村，由方形的朝水楼、阳照楼、永贵楼、永盛楼、永荣楼、绳庆楼和圆形的春贵楼、裕兴楼、裕昌楼、永庆楼、晓春楼、东升楼及世遗土楼中唯一呈五角形的南薰楼共 13 座土楼组成。

　　河坑土楼群中最古老的朝水楼，由张氏祖先始建于 1549 年，后子孙繁衍，在这个不足一平方千米的山间溪畔，建起了一座又一座土楼，形成福建土楼分布最密集的楼群。其中最年轻的永庆楼，建成于 20 世纪 60 年代。整个土楼群的建造时间足足跨越了 400 多年。

◎ 彩霞漫天映土楼。（冯木波 摄）
The cluster under rosy clouds. (Photo by Feng Mubo)

◎ 谜一样的土楼群。（冯木波 摄）
A riddle-like Tulou cluster. (Photo by Feng Mubo)

■ Hekeng Tulou Cluster in Nanjing

Hekeng Tulou Cluster is located in Hekeng Village, Shuyang Town in Zhangzhou City. There are 13 Tulou of both square and circular shapes, namely the square Chaoshuilou, Yangzhaolou, Yongguilou, Yongshenglou, Yongronglou, Shengqinglou, and the circular Chunguilou, Yuxinglou, Yuchanglou, Yongqinglou, Xiaochunlou, Dongshenglou, as well as Nanxunlou—the only Tulou in a pentagonal shape on the World Heritage List. The cluster is of Fujian's most densely populated Tulou. The Zhang's ancestors began to build Chaoshuilou around 1549, followed by Tulou being built one after another until Yongqinglou was completed in the 1960s. A time of over 400 years has witnessed the formation of the cluster.

■ 南靖云水谣景区

在云水谣景区山脚下、溪岸旁、田野上，星罗棋布着一座座姿态万千的土楼。这些土楼从13世纪元朝中期开始建造，目前保存完好的有53座。其中被列入《世界遗产名录》的，有建在沼泽地上堪称"天下第一奇"的和贵楼，有工艺精美、保护完好的双环圆形土楼怀远楼。此外，还有吊脚楼、竹竿楼、府第式土楼等，土楼风景别具一格。

■ Yunshuiyao Scenic Area in Nanjing

At Yunshuiyao Scenic Area many differently shaped Tulou buildings are scattered at the foot of the mountain, lining the bank of the river and sitting alongside fields. There are 53 well-preserved Tulou that have existed since the 13th century. Two of them can be found on UNESCO's World Heritage List, including Heguilou on marshland, known for being a wonder of the world, and the double-ringed Huaiyuanlou, known for its well-crafted design and meticulous preservation over the years. There are also other Tulou well-known for their very special shapes, such as stilt dwellings and mansion buildings.

◎ 建在沼泽地上的和贵楼。（胡家新 摄）
Heguilou built on marshland. (Photo by Hu Jiaxin)

和贵楼建于清代 1732 年，坐西朝东，占地面积 1,547 平方米，建筑面积 3,574 平方米。楼高 5 层，是列为世界文化遗产的福建土楼中"最高的方楼"。

和贵楼建在方圆 3,000 多平方米的沼泽地上，曾经用 200 多根直径 20 厘米的松木打桩、铺垫，历经 200 多年仍坚固稳定，巍然屹立。楼内共有 140 个房间，楼正中开一处大门，东西南北四方各有楼梯上下。由于该楼建在沼泽地上，游客在楼中的小天井里跺跺脚，就能感受到天井中整片鹅卵石的微微震动。

◎ 神奇的鹅卵石地面。（冯木波 摄）
Magical pebbled patio. (Photo by Feng Mubo)

Heguilou was built during the Qing Dynasty around 1732. It sits in the west and faces the east. The land area is 1,547 square metres while the building area is 3,574 square metres. It is five storeys high and is the tallest square Tulou listed on the UNESCO World Heritage List.

Heguilou was built on a 3,000-square-metre marshland. It used to be dotted with more than 200 pine trees with a diameter of almost 20 centimetres which have remained firm and stable for more than 200 years. There are 140 rooms in the building, an entrance in the middle and a staircase in the east, west, north and south side of the Tulou. Because Heguilou was built on marshland, you can feel the vibrations rumbling through the stones if you stamp your feet in the pebbled patio.

怀远楼是一座建于 1905 至 1909 年的双环圆形土楼，占地面积 1,384.7 平方米，建筑面积 3,468 平方米。楼顶屋檐下设有 4 个瞭望台，留有许多射击口，楼门正上方还设有 3 个防火灌水道。楼基以巨型鹅卵石和三合土垒筑，楼墙至今光整坚固，被视为古代生土夯筑技术研究的代表佳作。

The building structure of Huaiyuanlou consists of one circle within another and was built between 1905 and 1909. It covers a land area of 1,384.7 square metres and the building takes up an area of 3,468 square metres as a whole. There are four outlooks and many embrasures. There are also three fire prevention channels. The thick base was built with giant stones and reinforced with earth. The walls still have a smooth surface. It is regarded as the standard object for ancient earth architecture technology research.

◎ 怀远楼夜色。（冯木波 摄）
Night views of Huaiyuanlou. (Photo by Feng Mubo)

◎ 南阳楼倒影。（冯木波 摄）

Nanyanglou and its reflection. (Photo by Feng Mubo)

■ 华安大地土楼群

华安大地土楼群位于福建省漳州市华安县仙都镇大地村。大地村三面环山，两条小溪穿村而过，串起数十座土楼。其中二宜楼、南阳楼、东阳楼三座土楼是世界文化遗产"福建土楼"的组成部分。三座土楼为蒋氏祖孙在清朝所建，距今有200多年历史。

■ Dadi Tulou Cluster in Hua'an

Dadi Tulou Cluster can be found in Dadi Village in Hua'an County, Zhangzhou. Dozens of Tulou are located along the two streams running through the village, among which three Tulou are listed as the World Heritage sites. These three Tulou are Eryilou, Nanyanglou and Dongyanglou. They were built by the Jiang ancestors during the Qing Dynasty, having witnessed more than 200 years of history.

◎ 漳州"土楼之王"二宜楼。（王福平 摄）
Eryilou, the "Tulou King" in Zhangzhou. (Photo by Wang Fuping)

二宜楼是一座建于清乾隆五年（1740）的双环圆形土楼，占地面积 9,300 平方米，整座土楼分为 16 个单元。楼中心是一个占地约 600 平方米的大院子，设有 2 口水井。

二宜楼外墙厚达 2.53 米，底层外墙体有 12 个"之"字形传声洞，顶层设 1 米宽的环形外圈的"隐通廊"，将全楼连通。设观察窗和射击窗 56 个，枪眼 23 个。二宜楼的这种利用传声洞、泄沙漏水孔、秘密地下通道、隐通廊等构成的防卫系统，构思独特，堪称古代战略防御与民居生活完美结合的典范。

Eryilou is a double-ring Tulou built in 1740, taking up a land area of 9,300 square metres. The whole building is divided into 16 units. The inner courtyard is an area of 600 square metres for all residents and features two wells.

The outer wall of Eryilou is 2.53 metres thick. On the ground floor, the outer wall has 12 zigzag sound holes. The top floor was designed with a one-metre-wide corridor that connects the entire floor. It provides peripheral observation with 56 small windows to shoot arrows from, and 23 embrasures like openings for guns. The kind of defensive measures Eryilou was designed with, such as sound holes and secret underground passages, is a model of the perfect combination of the ancient strategic defence and ancient folk life.

泰宁丹霞
Taining Danxia

© 鸳鸯湖畔清晨暮鸟。（刘贤健摄）

Lovers' Peak at Mandarin Duck Lake. (Photo by Liu Xianjian)

遗产价值

　　中国丹霞是中国境内由陆相红色砂砾岩在内生力量（包括隆起）和外来力量（包括风化和侵蚀）共同作用下形成的各种地貌景观的总称。这一遗产包括中国西南部亚热带地区的 6 处遗产。它们的共同特点是壮观的赤壁丹崖以及一系列侵蚀地貌，如雄伟的天然岩柱、岩塔、沟壑、峡谷、瀑布等。这里跌宕起伏的地貌，对保护亚热带常绿阔叶林和包括约 400 种珍稀或濒危物种的动植物起到了重要作用。

　　中国丹霞作为自然遗产，于 2010 年 8 月被正式列入《世界遗产名录》。

◎ 大金湖畔大赤壁是中国最大的水上丹霞奇观。（刘贤健 摄）
Dachibi (the Grand Red Cliffs) by Dajin Lake is the largest Danxi spectacle over water in China. (Photo by Liu Xianjian)

Universal Value

China Danxia is the name given in China to landscapes developed on continental red terrigenous sedimentary beds influenced by endogenous forces (including uplift) and exogenous forces (including weathering and erosion). The inscribed site comprises six areas found in the sub-tropical zone of southwestern and southeastern China. They are characterized by spectacular red cliffs and a range of erosional landforms, including dramatic natural pillars, towers, ravines, valleys and waterfalls. These rugged landscapes have helped to conserve sub-tropical broad-leaved evergreen forests, and host many species of flora and fauna, about 400 of which are considered rare or threatened.

China Danxia was inscribed on the World Heritage List as a natural property in Aug. 2010.

"中国丹霞"是一个系列提名的世界自然遗产项目，由贵州赤水、福建泰宁、湖南崀山、广东丹霞山、江西龙虎山（龟峰）、浙江江郎山6个中国亚热带湿润区著名的丹霞地貌景区组成。

　　贵州赤水：青年早期——强抬升、深切割高原峡谷型丹霞的代表；

　　福建泰宁：青年晚期——深切割、山原峡谷曲流和多成因崖壁洞穴的代表；

　　湖南崀山：壮年早期——密集型圆顶、锥状丹霞峰丛峰林的代表；

　　广东丹霞山：壮年晚期——簇群式丹霞峰丛峰林的代表；

　　江西龙虎山（龟峰）：老年早期——疏散型丹霞峰林与孤峰群的代表；

　　浙江江郎山：老年晚期——高位孤峰型丹霞地貌的代表。

China Danxia consists of six famous Danxia landform tourist areas in the humid sub-tropical zone of China, namely, Chishui in Guizhou Province, Taining in Fujian Province, Mount Langshan in Hunan Province, Mount Danxia in Guangdong Province, Turtle Peak on Mount Longhu in Jiangxi Province, and Mount Jianglang in Zhejiang Province. Mountains, like human beings, will experience birth, growth, maturity, ageing and death.

Chishui in Guizhou Province: Early stage of the youth period—the representative of high elevation, topographic uplifting deep cutting Danxia canyons.

Taining in Fujian Province: Late stage of the youth period—the representative of deep mountain plateau canyons and multi-genesis cliff caves.

Mount Langshan in Hunan Province: Early stage of the prime period—the representative of peak clusters with intensive-dome or cone-shaped peaks.

Mount Danxia in Guangdong Province: Late stage of the prime period—the representative of cluster-type Danxia peaks.

Mount Longhu (Turtle Peak) in Jiangxi Province: Early stage of the senior period—the representative of spread-out Danxia peak forests and solitary peak groups.

Mount Jianglang in Zhejiang Province: Late stage of the senior period—the representative of high solitary peaks of Danxia landform.

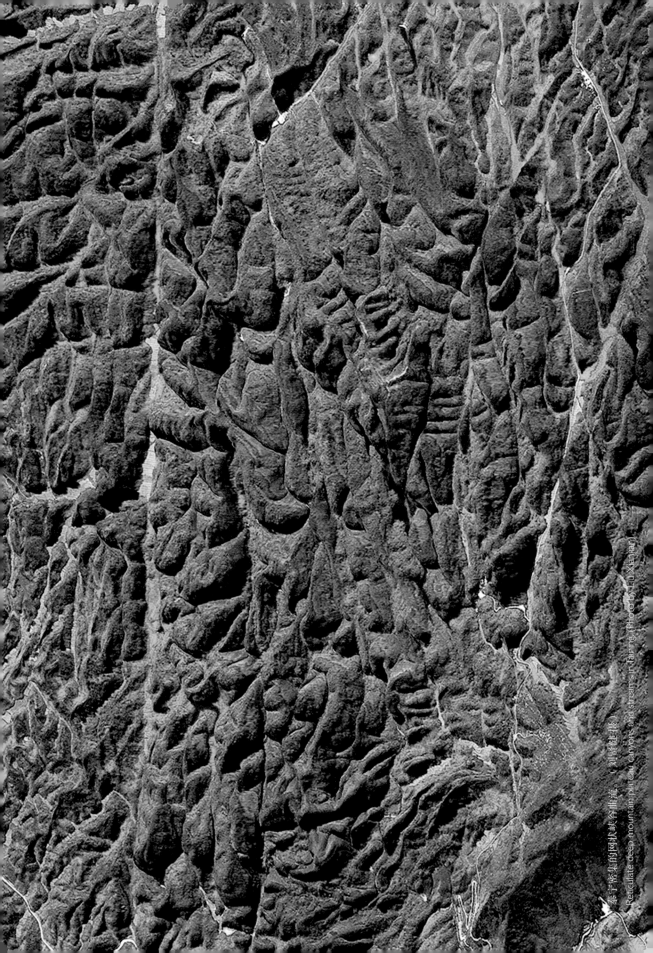

茶丁密集的网状峡谷地貌（太阳湖县城）

Reticulate deep mountain plateau, canyons and streams in Taining. (Photo by Liu Xianjian)

泰宁丹霞问奇

　　泰宁丹霞地貌区保存了清晰的古剥夷面，被密集的网状峡谷和巷谷分割为破碎的山原面；独特的崖壁洞穴群、密集的深切峡谷曲流和原始的沟谷生态构成其罕见的地质遗迹特征，成为青年期低海拔山原峡谷型丹霞地貌的代表；峡谷急流与密集峰丛紧密结合，山水景观优美；保持了生态环境的原生性、生物和生态多样性。

　　泰宁丹霞以"密集的网状谷地、发育的崖壁洞穴、完好的古夷平面、宏大的水上丹霞"，在"中国丹霞"系列遗产地中具有不可替代的地位，被冠以"水上丹霞园""峡谷大观园""洞穴博物馆"等美誉。

◎ 完好的古夷平面。（刘贤健 摄）
Intact ancient planation surface. (Photo by Liu Xianjian)

Exploring Taining Danxia

The Taining Danxia landform area maintains a clear ancient planation surface and an original mountain face which is divided into fragmentized surface by dense netlike canyons and U-shaped valleys. The unique cliff wall cave groups, the dense deep cutting canyons and meandering streams, and primitive gully ecology have formed rare natural features. It is the representative of low-altitude mountains and gorges of adolescent Danxia. The rapid streams in the canyon intertwine with dense peaks, which shapes the beautiful scenery of the mountains and streams. The primordial ecological environment and the bio-diversity are well preserved here.

Taining Danxia boasts "the most dense net-like valleys, the most full-grown cliff caves, the intact ancient planation surface, and the most magnificent Danxia landform on water". Taining Danxia plays an irreplaceable role in "China Danxia". It has many spectacle labels, such as "Water Danxia Garden", "Grand View Canyon Park" and "Cave Museum".

■ 丹霞崖壁

坡度大于 60 度、高度大于 10 米的丹霞陡崖坡，平地拔起，巍然高耸，比如大金湖上的大赤壁。

■ Danxia Cliffs

It is a kind of steep cliff with a slope that is greater than 60 degrees and a height that is over 10 meters. It rises straight from the ground and soars high. Dachibi by Dajin Lake is an example.

◎ 雄伟壮观的大赤壁是水上丹霞的典型代表。（刘贤健 摄）
The magnificent Dachibi is a typical Danxia cliff over water. (Photo by Liu Xianjian)

■ 丹霞方山

　　丹霞方山山顶平缓，四壁陡立，呈城堡状，往往只有一条小道可通达山顶。古人常利用方山筑寨，如黄石寨、南石寨、虎头寨等。

■ Danxia Mesas

Danxia mesas have flat tops and each has four steep sides, which look like castles. Each mesa usually only has one trail as access to the top. In ancient times, people often built villages or fortresses in these square-shaped mesas, such as the famous Huangshi (Yellow Stone) Fortress, Nanshi Fortress, and the Hutou (Tiger Head) Fortress.

◎ 隐身蓝天碧水间的黄石寨。（刘贤健 摄）
The Yellow Stone Fortress between blue water and sky. (Photo by Liu Xianjian)

■ 石峰石柱

　　泰宁丹霞地貌中有着发育良好的红层奇观——丹霞石峰、石柱。奇峰异柱，争奇斗艳。有的似情侣相依，如情侣峰；有的如仙人相聚，如八仙崖；有的如利剑出鞘，直指天空，如三剑峰。

■ Danxia Peaks and Pillars

Taining Danxia contains spectacular red-bed landforms that are well-developed, such as isolated peaks, towers and pillars. They are shaped in different forms and figures as if they try to compete for attention. The Lovers' Peak, for example, looks like two love birds snuggling up to each other. Baxianya (the Eight-Immortal Peaks) remind us a picture of several immortals gathering together. And the Three-Sword Peak got the name from the shape of the pillars.

◎ 三剑峰。（刘贤健 摄）
The Three-Sword Peak. (Photo by Liu Xianjian)

◎ "红装"素裹，分外妖娆。（刘贤健 摄）
The red Danxia peak looks more beautiful than ever when covered with snow. (Photo by Liu Xianjian)

■ 丹霞石墙

薄薄的呈长条状的山体，长度比宽度大两倍甚至数十倍，高度也大于宽度，像是一堵凌空降下的墙，壮观异常，如月老岩（也称老君岩）。

■ Danxia Stone Walls

This is a kind of thin and strip-shaped mountain with a length that is two to ten times larger than the width, and with a height that is greater than the width. It looks like a wall towering to the skies and the view is spectacular. Yuelao Rock (also called Laojun Rock) is a good example of the Danxia stone wall.

◎ 月老岩。（刘贤健 摄）
Yuelao Rock. (Photo by Liu Xianjian)

■ 崩积堆和崩积巨石

多在陡崖之下，因崖壁重力崩塌堆积而成，或堆积成山丘，或形成崩积洞穴，如寨下大峡谷的云崖岭。

■ Colluvia and Colluvial Giant Stones

The colluvia are mostly piled up or caved at the base of a cliff or slope. The reason behind the formation of colluvia is the effect of gravity. The giant stones at Yunya Ridge in the Zhaixia Grand Canyon is a kind of colluvial stones.

◎ 云崖岭崩积巨石。
（刘贤健 摄）
Colluvial stones at Yunya Ridge. (Photo by Liu Xianjian)

■ 丹霞沟谷

这是丹霞负地貌中最重要的景观，包括宽谷、峡谷、巷谷、线谷等，如一线天；因受流水侵蚀深切形成的曲流，如上清溪。

■ Danxia Valleys

This is the most important landscape of Danxia negative landforms, including wide valleys, canyons, ravines, U-shaped canyons, V-shaped canyons, such as a Sliver of Sky. Shangqing Stream is a meandering stream that has formed because of deep-cutting of water.

◎ 峡谷曲流。（刘贤健 摄）
Canyons and meandering streams. (Photo by Liu Xianjian)

◎ 幽谷迷津。（刘贤健 摄）

The Valley Maze. (Photo by Liu Xianjian)

◎ 百褶峡。（刘贤健 摄）

Baizhe (Hundred-Turning) Canyon. (Photo by Liu Xianjian)

◎ 圣丰岩独特的丹霞岩穴村落。（刘贤健 摄）
The unique village built inside Danxia rock cave at Shengfeng Rock. (Photo by Liu Xianjian)

■ 丹霞洞穴

　　丹霞洞穴成洞的部位多在软弱的岩层，软岩层相对快速的风化使之凹进，形成洞穴，主要有额状洞、扁平洞、拱形洞等类型，如状元岩、圣丰岩、甘露岩上的岩洞。

◎ 藏棺岩（为男性村民准备的棺木）。（刘贤健 摄）
The rock cave for hiding coffins prepared for male villagers. (Photo by Liu Xianjian)

■ Danxia Caves

Danxia caves are mostly formed in soft rock layers. The relatively rapid weathering makes the soft rock layer recess to form caves. These caves are mainly frontal caves, flat caves and other types such as the caves in Zhuangyuan Rock, Shengfeng Rock and Ganlu Rock.

■ 丹霞穿洞

其实这也是丹霞洞穴的一种。在丹霞岩层中，软岩地段先形成洞穴，日久天长，石墙被蚀穿，两边通透，就成了穿岩。穿岩如果被侵蚀，岩壁后退并不断垮塌，当跨度大于洞顶厚度的时候，就成为石拱。石拱横跨在河谷上的称天生桥，如大田读书山的天生桥。

■ Danxia Arches

This is also a kind of Danxia caves. The soft rock sections of the thin Danxia walls first form caves and over time, the thin walls are penetrated under the effect of erosion. An arch is formed when the two sides of the walls are hollow. If the rock is eroded, and when the span is longer than the thickness of the top of the cave, it becomes a stone arch. The stone arch across the river valley is called Tiansheng (meaning natural) Bridge, such as the Tiansheng Bridge in Datian Township.

◎ 少见的天生桥。（刘贤健 摄）
The rare Tiansheng Bridge. (Photo by Liu Xianjian)

■ 天穹岩

丹霞地貌中还有一种蜂窝状洞穴，是在崖壁上或洞穴顶部星罗棋布的细小洞穴，如同剖开的蜂房，如寨下大峡谷的天穹岩，属于丹霞微地貌的特殊景观。

■ The Sky-Dome Rock

There is also a kind of beehive-shaped cave, which are clusters of small caves on the cliff or on top of the cave, like an open hive. An example of the beehive-shaped cave is Tianqiong (the Sky-Dome) Rock at the Zhaixia Grand Canyon. This kind of cave is a special micro-landform of Danxia.

◎ 天穹岩。（刘贤健 摄）
The Sky-Dome Rock. (Photo by Liu Xianjian)

■ 自然之歌

　　泰宁以青年期丹霞地貌为主，兼有花岗岩、火山岩、构造地质地貌等多种地质遗迹，峡谷曲流多姿多彩。类型丰富的地质生态，也相应形成了复杂多样的生态环境，创造了各种植物生长、野兽栖息繁衍的条件，保存了全球性和地方性的珍稀濒危物种。

　　植物之中，有国家一级保护系列的银杏、南方红豆杉、伯乐树与东方水韭；列入国际自然保护联盟（IUCN）《红色名录》的有铁皮石斛、银钟花、黄山木兰、沉水樟、闽楠、红豆树、伞花木、伯乐树、银杏、长叶榧10种，其中铁皮石斛被列为极危物种；列入濒危野生动植物种国际贸易公约（CITES，又称华盛顿公约）附录保护目录的有金毛狗、石仙桃等65种。脊椎动物里，列入IUCN《红色名录》的有白颈长尾雉、鬣羚、豹、大灵猫等，列入CITES附录保护目录的有游隼、白颈长尾雉、金猫等。

◎ 长兴村的红豆树群。（刘贤健 摄）

Ormosia hosiei trees in Changxing Village. (Photo by Liu Xianjian)

■ The Songs of Nature

The landscape of Taining is mainly composed of youth Danxia landforms as well as granite, volcanic rock, tectonic geological landforms and other geological relics, together with diverse canyons, rivers and streams. The rich geological and ecological types have provided conditions for the growth of various plants and the reproduction of wild animals, preserving those rare and endangered species on a global and local scale.

Among the plants, ginkgo, Taxus chinensis, Bretschneidera sinensis and Isoetes orientalis are listed as the national first-class protection series; there are ten species in the Red List of Threatened Species of the International Union for Conservation of Nature (IUCN) including Dendrobium officinale, Halesia macgregorii chun, Magnolia cylindrica, Cinnamomum micranthum, Phoebe bournei, Ormosia hosiei, Eurycorymbus cavaleriei, Taxus chinensis, ginkgo, and Torreya jackii. Among them, Dendrobium officinale is listed as an extremely endangered species. There are sixty-five other species, such as Cibotium barometz and Chinese Pholidota Herb, listed in the appendix to The Convention on International Trade in Endangered Species of Wild Fauna and Flora (CITES) . Among vertebrates, those included in the Red List of IUCN are Syrmaticus ellioti, serow, leopard and zibet, while those listed in the the CITES appendix include peregrine falcon, Syrmaticus ellioti and golden cat.

◎ 东方水韭。（刘贤健 摄）
The Isoetes orientalis. (Photo by Liu Xianjian)

◎ 大田乡的千年银杏树。（刘贤健 摄）
A 1000-year-old ginkgo in Datian Township. (Photo by Liu Xianjian)

◎ 长叶榧。（刘贤健 摄）
A Torreya jackii. (Photo by Liu Xianjian)

◎ 闽楠树群。（刘贤健 摄）
The Phoebe bournei group. (Photo by Liu Xianjian)

◎ 勺鸡。（刘贤健 摄）

A pukras. (Photo by Liu Xianjian)

◎ 白颈长尾雉。（刘贤健 摄）

An Elliot's pheasant. (Photo by Liu Xianjian)

◎ 黄腹角雉。（刘贤健 摄）

A Cabot's tragopan. (Photo by Liu Xianjian)

鼓浪屿：历史国际社区

Kulangsu: a Historic International Settlement

从鹭江眺望对岸夜色（林乔森 摄）

City night across the Lujiang Strait. (Photo by Lin-Qiaosen)

遗产价值

　　鼓浪屿位于福建九龙江入海口，与厦门岛隔海相望。随着 1843 年厦门开辟为通商口岸和 1903 年鼓浪屿成为国际社区，这座位于中国南方海岸线上的小岛突然成了中外交流的重要窗口。鼓浪屿是中西文化交流融合的特例。鼓浪屿有机的城市肌理清晰地保留了其发展变化的痕迹，见证了数十年间多元文化不断融入当地文化的过程。岛上拥有包括传统闽南建筑、西方古典复兴建筑和殖民地外廊式建筑等不同的建筑风格。从鼓浪屿兴起的厦门装饰风格融合了 20 世纪早期的现代风格和装饰艺术，是文化间影响融合最突出的证明。"鼓浪屿：历史国际社区"作为文化遗产于 2017 年 7 月被列入《世界遗产名录》。

© 天风海涛鼓浪屿。（林乔森摄）
Kulangsu in between the sky and the sea. (Photo by Lin Qiaosen)

◎ 鹭江两岸。（林乔森 摄）
Kulangsu and Amoy across the Lujiang Strait. (Photo by Lin Qiaosen)

Universal Value

Kulangsu (also known as Gulangyu) is a tiny island located on the estuary of the Jiulongjiang (Chiu-lung) River, opposite the city of Amoy (now Xiamen). With the opening of a commercial port at Amoy in 1843, and the establishment of the island as an international settlement in 1903, this island off the southern coast of China suddenly became an important window for Sino-foreign exchanges. Kulangsu is an exceptional example of the cultural integration that emerged from these exchanges, which remains woven into its urban fabric. There is a mixture of different architectural styles including the traditional South Fujian Style, Western Classical Revival Style and Veranda Colonial Style. The most clearest testimony to this fusion of various stylistic influences is a new architectural movement, the Amoy Deco Style, which is a synthesis of the Modernist Style of the early 20th century and Art Deco. Kulangsu, as a Historic International Settlement and a culture heritage, was inscribed on the World Heritage List in July, 2017.

© 覆鼎岩上的郑成功塑像 （康伦恩 摄）
Statue of Koxinga (Zheng Chenggong) on Fuding Rock. (Photo by Kang Lun'en)

鼓浪撷英

■ 天风海涛——自然景观与文化遗迹

　　鼓浪屿，最初不过是个无人的小小荒岛，孤悬于茫茫大海中。因为形呈椭圆，鼓浪屿最初得名"圆洲仔"。

　　在鼓浪屿无惊无扰的渔猎耕种岁月里，明末清初郑成功率领他的军队来到岛上，辟此为揭牙之地，屯营扎寨，操练水兵。在彼时，小岛也曾是郑氏开展海上贸易的基地之一。

　　海拔92.68米的日光岩是鼓浪屿的最高点，亦是鼓浪屿的必游之地。历朝历代的摩崖题刻汇集在日光岩的各处，成为人文胜景

◎ 日光岩上有历朝历代的摩崖石刻。（康伦恩 摄）
Cliff inscriptions of past generations on Sunlight Rock (Photo by Kang Lun'en)

◎ 日光岩景区。（林乔森 摄）

Sunlight Rock Scenic Spot. (Photo by Lin Qiaosen)

The Beauty of Kulangsu

■ Paradise on Earth: A Collection of Natural and Cultural Wonders

Kulangsu used to be a desolate island just off the coast and was originally named "Yuanzhouzi" (Round Sandbank) after its oval shape.

The peaceful days of fishing, hunting and farming were no more when Koxinga and his troops garrisoned on Kulangsu during the late Ming and early Qing dynasties. They used the place as a fort to train naval forces, as well as a base for maritime trade.

With an elevation of 92.68 meters, Sunlight Rock is the highest elevation point on Kulangsu and a must-visit destination for tourists. It is also known for its cliff inscriptions by famous people throughout history.

■ 文化交融——公共地界与国际社区

随着 1843 年厦门的开埠、1903 年鼓浪屿公共地界的确立以及随后华侨归国定居的热潮，在中西文化的合力之下，鼓浪屿蜕变成一个世所瞩目的岛屿。

1845 年，一位叫德滴的苏格兰商人在厦门开设德记洋行后，和记、宝记、旗昌、美时、瑞记等洋行相继开办。洋行的经营地点在厦门，会所和住宅则设鼓浪屿。

1863 年，英国在鼓浪屿的领事馆落成，英国领事也正式从厦门搬到鼓浪屿办公。西班牙、法国、美国、德国、日本等国的领事馆也相继在鼓浪屿落成。

◎ 鼓浪屿上的美国领事馆旧址。（陈亚元 供图）
Site of the US Consulate on Kulangsu. (Courtesy of Chen Yayuan)

◎ 19 世纪 70 年代的鼓浪屿。（白桦 供图）
Kulangsu in the 1870s. (Courtesy of Bai Hua)

■ Cultural Integration: Public Land and International Settlement

After Amoy was opened as one of the treaty ports in 1843 and in 1903, the International Settlement of Kulangsu was established, followed by an upsurge of overseas Chinese returning to China and settling down on Kulangsu. As a result of the joint influence of Chinese and Western cultures, the island began to draw worldwide attention.

In 1845, a Scottish merchant named James Tait set up Tait & Co. in Amoy. Other foreign firms were established afterwards, such as Boyd & Co., Pasedag & Co., Russell & Co., Milisch & Co. and Lessler & Co. They operated in Amoy but had their private clubs and residences on Kulangsu.

In 1863, construction of the British Consulate on Kulangsu was completed, and the British Consul moved his office from Amoy to Kulangsu. Consulates of Spain, France, the United States, Germany, Japan and other countries were also established on the island.

　　1902年1月10日，中外代表在日本驻厦门领事馆签署了《厦门鼓浪屿公共地界章程》。1902年11月21日，光绪皇帝批准鼓浪屿正式成为公共地界。1903年1月，鼓浪屿公共地界工部局成立。

On January 10, 1902, representatives of China and foreign countries signed *Land Regulations for the Settlement of Kulangsu, Amoy*, at the Japanese Consulate in Amoy. On November 21, 1902, Emperor Guangxu approved Kulangsu to be an international settlement. In January 1903, the Kulangsu Municipal Council was established.

◎ 鼓浪屿巡捕局巡捕合影。（白桦 供图）
The Kulangsu Muncipal Police, Amoy. (Courtesy of Bai Hua)

19 世纪末，台湾被日本占领，许多台湾富商内渡鼓浪屿，这其中有台湾两大家族，板桥林家和雾峰林家。

1920 年至 1930 年，早年下南洋发家致富的闽南移民纷纷入住鼓浪屿。这是因为鼓浪屿的居住环境宜人、教育以及文化氛围优良。加之鼓浪屿与其家乡生活习俗相近，语言相通，且有公共地界的安全护佑、工部局现代化的社区管理，南洋华侨纷纷在鼓浪屿这个宜居之地修建华屋，安家置业。

◎ 借山藏海的菽庄花园。（康伦恩 摄）
Shuzhuang Garden Villa in between the hill and the sea. (Photo by Kang Lun'en)

◎ 鼓浪屿第一条带骑楼的商业街（今龙头路）。（康伦恩 摄）
The first commercial street lined with arcade buildings on Kulangsu, now Longtou Road. (Photo by Kang Lun'en)

At the end of the 19th century, Taiwan was occupied by Japanese invaders. Many business people there moved to the mainland and settled down on Kulangsu. Among them were two Lin families from Banchiau and Wufong.

Between 1920 and 1930, immigrants from South Fujian who had moved to Southeast Asian countries and made a fortune there returned to settle down on Kulangsu owing to the island's pleasant living environment, excellent education and cultural atmosphere. The pleasant day-to-day life, language spoken, security guarantee in the international settlement and the modern community management by the Municipal Council attracted many overseas Chinese to take Kulangsu as an ideal place to build their mansions and villas.

■ 万国建筑——一席流动的盛宴

　　完好地保留着中外各种建筑风格之建筑的鼓浪屿，有"万国建筑博览园"之誉。岛上现存的 900 余栋历史风貌建筑，是鼓浪屿作为世界文化遗产的主要元素。

　　在 19 世纪中叶到 20 世纪中叶的百年间，鼓浪屿是东亚和东南亚区域独具特色的对外交流窗口。闽南传统风格、殖民地外廊式、西方古典复兴式、现代主义风格、装饰艺术风格等建筑风格汇聚于一座小岛，并在多元文化交流的土壤中生发出具有本土建筑特征的"厦门装饰风格"，影响辐射到沿海其他区域。

◎ 深红色的半球形穹顶是八卦楼的标志。（林乔森 摄）
The round tower on the top adorned by the impressive crimson domed roof: an iconic feature of Bagua Mansion. (Photo by Lin Qiaosen)

■ Rich Diversity of Architectural Styles: A Feast for the Eye

There are so many architectural masterpieces of both Chinese and Western styles here, which are kept intact and earn Kulangsu the moniker of "An Exhibition of the World's Architecture". Over 900 such buildings surviving today are a major factor of Kulangsu's status as a world cultural heritage site.

Kulangsu was once a unique gateway to the outside world, where exchanges between the East Asia and Southeast Asia took place during the hundred-year spanning from the mid-19th to mid-20th centuries. The place is itself an amalgamation of Eastern and Western architectural styles, including the traditional South Fujian Style, Veranda Colonial Style, Western Classical Revival Style, Modernist Style, Art Deco Style and other styles. It is from this coexistence of diverse cultures that the distinctive local "Amoy Deco Style" developed and grew, which has now spread along the coastline.

◎ 金瓜楼拥有两个标志性的穹顶。（林乔森 摄）
Golden Pumpkin Villa with two symbolic domes. (Photo by Lin Qiaosen)

闽南传统红砖民居

　　四落大厝，是鼓浪屿现存规模最大、保存最完整的一组闽南红砖厝建筑群，亦是岛上现存最古老的建筑群之一。大夫第是鼓浪屿现存最古老的红砖厝民居之一。

South Fujian Style Traditional Red-Brick Dwellings

The Four-Compound Mansion is, as of now, the largest and best preserved group of red brick residences of South Fujian Style as well as one of the oldest extant complexes on the island. Dafu Mansion is one of the oldest red-brick residential dwellings on Kulangsu.

◎ 四落大厝位于鼓浪屿中华路 23 号、25 号和海坛路 33 号、35 号至 39 号。（林乔森 摄）
The Four-Compound Mansion located at 23, 25 Zhonghua Road, 33 and 35-39 of Haitan Road, Kulangsu. (Photo by Lin Qiaosen)

◎ 建于悬崖之上的汇丰银行公馆旧址。（林乔森 摄）
Site of the residence of HSBC's President on the cliff. (Photo by Lin Qiaosen)

殖民地外廊式建筑

　　外国人在鼓浪屿占据风景优美之地，大兴土木。他们兴建的基本上是殖民地外廊式建筑，其风格便是具有休闲功能的外廊空间。殖民地外廊式建筑形成于南亚殖民地区，又于 18 世纪末 19 世纪初传回欧洲，并成为富裕阶层的郊野别墅样式。

Veranda Colonial Architectural Style

Foreigners have taken up construction projects in and around scenic areas of the island. Most buildings were built in the Veranda Colonial Style, of which the veranda was a place for leisure activities. This architectural style came into being in colonies in South Asia, and was introduced to Europe in country villas for the rich in the late 18th and early 19th centuries.

西方古典复兴风格及其他风格建筑

　　虽然 19 世纪中叶到 20 世纪初鼓浪屿上兴建的建筑基本是殖民地外廊式风格，但其中还有西方古典复兴式风格及其他风格的建筑，比如建于 1917 年的天主堂，是厦门地区仅存的一座哥特式天主教堂。另外还有协和礼拜堂、三一堂、安献堂等。

Western Classical Revival Architecture and Other Styles

Although buildings of Veranda Colonial Style prevailed in the period between the mid-19th and early 20th centuries on Kulangsu, there were Western Classical Revival Architecture and other styles. For instance, the Catholic Church is now the only existing Catholic church of the Gothic Style in the Amoy region. There are also the Union Church, the Trinity Church and Anxian Hall, etc, in the same style.

◎ 天主堂。（杨戈 摄）
Catholic Church. (Photo by Yang Ge)

◎ 海天堂构中楼。（杨戈 摄）
Central building of Hai Tian Tang Gou Mansion. (Photo by Yang Ge)

"厦门装饰风格" 的萌发与兴盛

在闽、台的富绅及闽籍华侨定居鼓浪屿的热潮中，鼓浪屿在多元文化交流的土壤中生发出具有本土建筑特征的"厦门装饰风格"。

这种由西方古典复兴式、现代主义风格、装饰艺术风格融合生发出的建筑风格，呈现在华侨建造的具有本土特征的华侨洋楼、华侨家族宅园、私家园林中，并且成为鼓浪屿的"万国建筑"中华丽而珍贵的存在。

Popularization and Growth of the Amoy Deco Style

While there was an increasing number of mansions constructed by rich people of Fujian and Taiwan, and overseas Chinese from Fujian settling down on Kulangsu, Amoy Deco Style, a localized architectural style, had its roots taken hold in the soil of cultural diversity.

It is a combination of Western Classical Revival Style, Modernist Style and Art Deco Style together with local features typically found in houses, mansions and private gardens, which have been magnificent and valuable presence of the diversified architectural styles on Kulangsu.

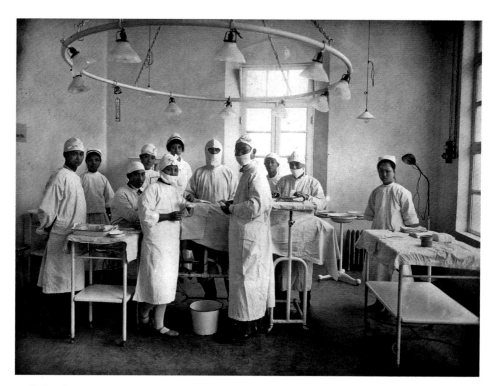

◎ 救世医院的医生和护士。（白桦 供图）

Doctors and nurses of Hope Hospital. (Courtesy of Bai Hua)

■ 外来宗教——左手医疗，右手教育

在厦门成为《南京条约》签署后首批开放的口岸前，鼓浪屿就成了基督教传教士的大本营。教育与医疗，既是教会不可或缺的深入当地的途径，也使鼓浪屿的居民率先得到现代医疗的庇护，以及可以较早接受先进的教育。

■ Foreign Religions: Spreading the Gospel Through Medicine and Education

Even before Amoy was opened as one of the first commercial ports with the *Treaty of Nanking (Nanjing)*, Kulangsu had already been a stronghold for Christian missionaries. Education and medicine were not only indispensable for the church to take root on Kulangsu, but also beneficial to local residents.

1842 年 6 月 7 日，美国归正教会在鼓浪屿开设了一个小型的诊所，这是厦门的第一家西医诊所。救世医院则是鼓浪屿第一座医院，也曾是闽南最大的综合性医院，它的建立为厦门乃至福建及东南亚带来了现代意义上的医学技术、医疗设备和医疗服务。

On June 7, 1842, the American Reformed Church opened a clinic on Kulangsu, which was the first Western medicine clinic in Amoy. Hope Hospital was the first hospital on Kulangsu and the biggest general hospital in South Fujian. Its establishment had brought to Amoy, Fujian and even Southeast Asia modern medical technology, equipment and services.

◎ 救世医院旧址。（林乔森 摄）
Former Hope Hospital. (Photo by Lin Qiaosen)

从 19 世纪 50 年代到公共地界时期，传教士在鼓浪屿上兴办起各种各样的学校：幼儿园、小学、中学、师范、专门的医学校、职业学校、神学院……

鼓浪屿的中、小学校数量之多，其密度之高，居于全国前列，并且在闽南、台湾以及东南亚等地颇有影响。

From the 1850s until the establishment of the international settlement, missionaries set up various schools on Kulangsu such as kindergartens, primary schools, high schools, teachers' schools, specialized medical schools, vocational schools, seminaries...

There was a high density of secondary and primary schools despite the size of Kulangsu. This also added to the influence of Kulangsu in South Fujian, Taiwan and Southeast Asia.

◎ 1892 年美国归正教牧师与田尾女学堂学生合影。（白桦 供图）

Missionaries of American Reformed Church with students of Tianwei Girls' School, 1892. (Courtesy of Bai Hua)

◎ 鼓浪屿风琴博物馆的镇馆之宝——卡萨翁第 700 号管风琴。（朱庆福 摄）
Casavant Opus 700 pipe organ, one of the most impressive highlights of Kulangsu Organ Museum. (Photo by Zhu Qingfu)

■ 音乐体育——永不止息的回响

"琴岛"，是鼓浪屿的别称。西洋音乐来到鼓浪屿，首先是以宗教音乐的形式出现。

1878 年，协和礼拜堂的礼拜开始使用管风琴。1913 年，林尔嘉从欧洲买了一架真正的钢琴，用作家居装饰陈列。这便是鼓浪屿第一架钢琴。

随着西人脚步的踏足，西方近代体育运动也来到了鼓浪屿。赛马、高尔夫球、保龄球最早传入中国都是在鼓浪屿。英华书院在 1898 年成立福建省第一支足球队，同时也是中国近代第一支足球队。

■ Ongoing Glory: Island of Music and Sports

"Piano Island" is another name for Kulangsu. Western music on Kulangsu started in the form of religious music. In 1878, Union Church began to use the organ to accompany the choir. In 1913, Lin Erjia (Lim Nee Kar) bought a real piano from Europe, and put it to use as home decor. This was the first piano on Kulangsu.

Together with Westerners who set their foot on Kulangsu, modern Western sports such as horse race, golf and bowling were first introduced into China on Kulangsu. In 1898, the first football team in Fujian Province and in modern China on the whole was founded in the Anglo-Chinese College (Yinghua Academy).

© 1932 年毓德女中排球队参加厦门排球锦标赛。（白桦 供图）
Volleyball team of Loktek Girl's School at Amoy Volleyball Championship, in 1932. (Courtesy of Bai Hua)

泉州：宋元中国的世界海洋商贸中心

Quanzhou: Emporium of the World in Song-Yuan China

遗产价值

　　泉州曾是 10 至 14 世纪世界海洋贸易网络中高度繁荣的商贸中心之一，作为宋元中国与世界的对话窗口，展现了中国完备的海洋贸易制度体系、发达的经济水平以及多元包容的文化态度。22 处代表性古迹遗址及其关联环境，分布在自海港经江口平原并一直延伸到腹地山区的广阔空间内，它们完整地体现了宋元泉州富有特色的海外贸易体系与多元社会结构，多维度地支撑了"宋元中国的世界海洋商贸中心"这一价值主题。

Universal Value

Quanzhou was one of the prosperous key commercial centres of the world maritime trade network during the 10th and 14th centuries. A window of dialogue between China and the rest of the world during the Song and Yuan dynasties, it was an example of China's complex maritime trade network, developed economy, and inclusive culture. There are twenty-two exemplary historical sites found across the vast expanse of Quanzhou, their locations ranging from harbours to the estuarine plains and mountain ranges across the city. These cultural sites are remnants that prove the distinctive overseas trade system of Quanzhou during the Song and Yuan dynasties and the pluralistic society structure, thus giving Quanzhou the title "Emporium of the World in Song-Yuan China".

© 古城泉州夜景。（陈英杰 摄）
A night view of the ancient city Quanzhou. (Photo by Chen Yingjie)

◎ 开元寺东西塔作为中国最高的一对石塔，已成为历史文化名城泉州的标志。（许师伟 摄）

As the highest twin pagodas in China, the East Pagoda and the West Pagoda of Kaiyuan Temple have become the landmark of Quanzhou, a famous historical and cultural city. (Photo by Xu Shiwei)

千年商港回望

　　泉州——一座闪烁着中世纪海上丝绸之路文明之光的城市。

　　早在公元八世纪初，晋江入海口已兴起一座港口小城。随着海外贸易的迅速发展，短短两百多年之后，这个以刺桐之名为人所知的地方，已经成为中国南方最大的商港之一。当其鼎盛时期，她是远航异域的出发之地，也是招徕番商的"光明之城"；她是中世纪旅行家眼中的"东方第一大港"，更是宋元中国的世界海洋商贸中心。

A Look back at the Millenary Port of Quanzhou

Quanzhou was a gleaming beacon of prosperity on the Maritime Silk Road during the Middle Ages.

By the beginning of the 8th century, a small port city had sprung up at the estuary of Jinjiang River. Due to the rapid development of maritime trade, only two centuries later, it had grown to be one of the largest and well-known commercial ports in southern China, named Zayton. In its prime, Quanzhou was the point of departure for overseas ventures, and a haven of light for merchants. It was regarded as the largest port in the East for travellers at the time, and Song-Yuan China's maritime world trade centre.

■ 招商入番　祈风祭海

　　公元946年，清源军节度使留从效拓建泉州城，环城遍植刺桐，泉州城因此又被称为刺桐城。但真正带给刺桐城生命力的，是能给从事贸易的海商带来实在利益的新政策、新机构。

■ Attracting Merchants to Quanzhou's Shores and Worshipping the Wind and Sea Gods

In 946, Liu Congxiao ordered the planting of many erythrina trees in Quanzhou, which led it to be known as Erythrina Tree City. This nickname, through the Arabic translation, became romanized to Zayton. Zayton City was special because of the introduction of new policies and institutions that benefited the merchants and rewarded maritime trade, a trade that greatly vitalized the city.

◎ 泉州东湖公园里的刺桐花。（陈英杰 摄）
The erythrina flowers in Quanzhou's East Lake Park. (Photo by Chen Yingjie)

◎ 泉州市舶司遗址。（陈英杰 摄）

The former site of the Maritime Trade Office of Quanzhou. (Photo by Chen Yingjie)

市舶司遗址

市舶司，"掌蕃货、海舶、征榷、贸易之事，以来远人，通远物"。北宋元祐二年（1087），宋哲宗正式下令在泉州设立市舶司。从此，泉州也可独立处理海上贸易，拥有了区域经济的自主权。泉州市舶司的设立，使泉州港的海商和船民可以就地申办手续，并合法地回帆本港住舶。南宋时期，市舶收入充实日渐匮乏的国库，因而南宋朝廷对海外贸易更为重视，既扩大了泉州市舶司的职权，也进一步加强了对泉州市舶的扶持。

Site of the Maritime Trade Office

In 1087 during the Northern Song Dynasty, Emperor Zhezong ordered the establishment of the Maritime Trade Office in Quanzhou, responsible for handling imports, marine traffic, taxes, other trade issues and foreign travellers. This empowered Quanzhou to manage its own trade and granted its regional economy some autonomy. Merchants and sailors were also able to handle customs procedures on the spot and legally anchor their ships. During the Southern Song Dynasty, the increasingly scarce national treasury relied on the income from the Maritime Trade Office, drawing more attention to the prosperity of maritime trade, resulting in an enlarged authority and power of the office and a priority being placed upon the development of economic activities in Quanzhou.

南外宗正司遗址

两宋时代，福建是远离兵燹的后方，又是"田赋登足"、外贸活跃的富庶之地，因此引来大批皇室宗亲。南外宗正司的迁入，带来了皇权，也带来了中原先进的技艺。而南外宗正司的庞大开销由泉州地方政府、福建转运使司和泉州市舶司供给，这种财政负担和政治压力转化为官方对海外贸易增长的企盼。皇家宗室子弟既是特权消费集团，也同时参与海外商业活动。这些都刺激了泉州海外贸易的增长。

Site of Southern Clan Office

During the Northern and Southern Song dynasties, Fujian was a long way from the ravages of war and a place of abundant land taxes and active overseas trade, making it highly attractive as a getaway for the royal family. The royal family brought with them advanced technology of the Central Plain of China and the presence of imperial power. The huge expenses incurred by the royal family fell upon the Quanzhou local government, the Fujian Transport Office, and the Maritime Trade Office, once again drawing the attention of the government to the growth of overseas trade. Furthermore, the royal family were not simply a privileged group of wealthy individuals—they were also merchants in their own right, involved in overseas trade ventures. All these had significant impacts on the growth of Quanzhou's foreign trade network.

◎ 南宋建炎三年（1129）十二月，南外宗正司奉命率宗属三百多人从镇江迁驻泉州。（高能 摄）
In December of 1129, the Southern Clan Office ordered the relocation of over three hundred people from Zhenjiang to Quanzhou. (Photo by Gao Neng)

九日山祈风石刻

随着海上贸易在国家财政体系中的地位和影响日渐扩大，国家对海上贸易的管控和倡导也日益加强。祈风，祭海，也逐渐从民间行为转化为由官方主导。

九日山祈风石刻是迄今发现最为重要的祈风资料和物证，其中 10 方最为珍贵，记载了泉州市舶司和地方政府官员的 11 次祈风，最早的为 1174 年，最晚的为 1266 年。

Jiuri Mountain Wind-Praying Inscriptions

As maritime trade became a larger part of the country's economy, China devoted more time and resources to further controlling and strengthening it. Although the act of praying for propitious winds and offering sacrifices to the sea were initially something that the ordinary folk did, the government adopted the practices, and they eventually were primarily run by state officials. The stone carvings at Jiuri Mountain are the best preserved and most important material evidence of wind-praying discovered thus far. Of the carvings at this site, ten are particularly important, recording 11 sessions of prayer led by Quanzhou Maritime Trade Office and local government officials during 1174 and 1266.

◎ 祈风仪式的周期大致固定：孟夏四月举行回舶祈风，祈祷西南信风助归港船舶顺利回航；冬季十月到十二月举行遣舶祈风，祈祷东北信风送出海商船顺利远航。（陈英杰 摄）

There is an approximate cycle to praying for propitious winds: prayers in lunar April for the southwest wind to help ships return safely to ports, and prayers starting from lunar October to December for strong northeast winds to ensure smooth sailing far. (Photo by Chen Yingjie)

◎ 真武殿。（罗春日 摄）
Zhenwu Hall. (Photo by Luo Chunri)

真武庙、天后宫

　　祈风之外，还有祭海。始建于宋代的真武庙，位于内港法石村的石头山上，为一组依山势而筑的院落式建筑群，曾是"泉郡守望祭海神之所"，体现了政府对海洋贸易的鼓励与推动。

　　到元代，规模更大、影响更深的祭海神庙则为天后宫。天后宫位于泉州古城南，创建于 1196 年，始称顺济宫。宋代，官方在九日山延福寺祈风，商民在顺济庙奉祀妈祖，天后宫仍是民间庙宇，影响有限；到元代，泉州天后宫多次受到朝廷正式敕封，地方官员则每年致祭。

福建的文化与自然遗产
Cultural and Natural Heritage in Fujian

Zhenwu Temple and Tianhou Temple

In addition to praying for propitious winds, sacrifices were also made to the sea. Zhenwu Temple, built during the Song Dynasty, is located in the area of the ancient port of Fashi, on the foothills of Stone Hill. A group of courtyard structures leaning into the mountainous landscape, it was once the place of worship for the god of the sea and is an example of the commitment of the local government to encouraging and promoting maritime trade.

During the Yuan Dynasty, the larger and more influential temple to offer sacrifices to the god of the sea was Tianhou Temple. It is located on the southern end of the ancient city of Quanzhou. Originally constructed in 1196, it was first called Shunji Temple. During the Song Dynasty, officials prayed for favourable winds at Yanfu Temple on Jiuri Mountain, while merchants worshipped Matsu (Mazu), at Shunji Temple, which was of less influence at the time. It was during the Yuan Dynasty that Tianhou Temple was officially recognised by the royal court, and local officials began to pay their respects there annually.

◎ 天后宫正殿。（陈英杰 摄）
The main hall of Tianhou Temple. (Photo by Chen Yingjie)

■ 物华天宝　誉满十洲

　　自刺桐港于晚唐崛起，在海上贸易的带动下，泉州周边的地方手工业也日渐兴起，陶瓷、铜铁等制造业的发展尤为蓬勃。中国陶瓷品质优良、经久耐用，在海外广受欢迎；海上贸易兴起后，因其适宜于船运，又是海舶理想的压舱货物，陶瓷海外贸易变得十分兴盛，以外销为主的陶瓷业在刺桐港周边勃兴。晋江磁灶窑是泉州城郊规模最大的一组古窑址。

■ Land of Abundant Treasure and Wealth

The rise of Quanzhou Port in the late Tang Dynasty driven by maritime trade drove demand for locally produced goods around Quanzhou. This included works of ceramics, copper, and iron. Chinese ceramics were known to be of high quality and durability, making them popular overseas. Furthermore, its suitability for shipping as ballast cargo over maritime trade routes made ceramics a lucrative export, resulting in the industry flourishing around Quanzhou Port. Jinjiang Cizao Kiln is the largest group of ancient kiln sites in Quanzhou suburb.

◎ 金交椅山窑址。（成冬冬 摄）
Jinjiaoyishan Kiln Site (Cizao Kilns). (Photo by Cheng Dongdong)

◎ 德化屈斗宫窑址。（成冬冬 摄）

Dehua Qudougong Kiln Site. (Photo by Cheng Dongdong)

磁灶窑址、德化窑址

磁灶溪口山窑是南朝至唐代的遗址，出土的壶、盘等施青绿釉，已达到较高水平。宋元时期窑址多分布于晋江支流九十九溪两岸的小山坡上，以金交椅山窑址最为兴盛。磁灶窑出土的陶瓷多为青瓷、酱釉瓷，釉色丰富，以日用器为主。

德化，号称"世界瓷都"。德化窑始于晚唐，窑址遍布全县。德化窑生产的陶瓷可由陆路运输至永春，再经晋江支流东溪运往泉州港。德化窑除烧制影青器物外，以白瓷享有盛誉。德化窑烧造的产品在东亚、东南亚、南亚、西亚、东非等地区都有出土。

Cizao Kiln Sites and Dehua Kiln Sites

Cizao Xikoushan Kiln is a kiln site that was in use from the Southern Dynasty to the Tang Dynasty. Unearthed pots and plates were covered with a green glaze, and the ceramics were of a high quality. During the Song and Yuan dynasties, kiln sites were most often located on hillsides, particularly on the banks of the Jiushijiu Creek, a tributary of the Jinjiang River. The ceramics unearthed from the Cizao kiln sites are mostly celadon or glazed porcelain household items.

Dehua is known as the "Porcelain Capital of the World". Dehua kilns began in the late Tang Dynasty, springing up all over the county. The ceramics produced at the Dehua kiln sites were transported via land-based trade routes to Yongchun, before being loaded onto ships and transported over the East Creek, a tributary of the Jinjiang River, to Quanzhou Port. In addition to light celadon pieces, Dehua was known for its pristine white porcelain. Products made at Dehua kilns have been found in East Asia, Southeast Asia, South Asia, West Asia and East Africa.

安溪青阳下草埔冶铁遗址

安溪青阳下草埔冶铁遗址是宋元时期泉州冶铁手工业的珍贵见证，与泉州的陶瓷生产基地共同显示出宋元泉州强大的产业能力和贸易输出能力。青阳村曾是宋代官方设立的专职铁场之一。当时，人们使用小高炉进行块炼铁冶炼，并以木炭为主要燃料。生产的海绵铁经过初锻形成铁块、铁片等初加工制品后，再加工或运输至其他地区进行锻造成型，制成铁器。

◎ 下草埔遗址位于青阳村南部的山坡上，是宋代的块炼铁遗址。（刘伯怡 摄）
Located on the hillside south of Qingyang Village, Xiacaopu Site is an iron production site from the Song Dynasty. (Photo by Liu Boyi)

Xiacaopu Iron Production Site of Qingyang Village in Anxi

The Xiacaopu Iron Production Site is precious proof of the iron working industry in Quanzhou during the Song and Yuan dynasties. Together with the ceramic production sites, it is strong evidence that Quanzhou's industrial and trade capacity was significant during this time. Qingyang Village was once one of the key iron production sites established during the Song Dynasty. At the time, workers applied small blast furnaces fuelled by charcoal to smelt iron. The liquid iron was then forged to form iron blocks, sheets, or other preliminary products before being processed or transported elsewhere for forging.

◎ 美山码头。（陈英杰 摄）
Meishan Wharf. (Photo by Chen Yingjie)

◎ 文兴码头。（陈英杰 摄）
Wenxing Wharf. (Photo by Chen Yingjie)

■ 梯航万国　无远不至

刺桐港海外贸易的扩大，不仅为基础设施建设积累了资金，也对港口建设和经济腹地商品的集散提出了更高要求。整治泊港，铺路修桥，在两宋时期尤为突出，反映了海洋贸易给泉州社会带来的经济繁荣和财富积累。

■ The Path to Foreign Countries

The expansion of trade operations in Quanzhou Port resulted in an accumulation of funds that could be used for infrastructure development, but also increased the need for port construction, as well as a better inland trade network. A large amount of work was done during the Song Dynasty to renovate ports, pave roads, and build bridges, a reflection of the prosperity and wealth brought to Quanzhou by maritime trade.

江口码头

江口码头是泉州城郊的重要内港"法石港"的遗存，位于古城东南、晋江北岸，是连接古城的水陆转运节点。这里保存着文兴和美山两处码头以及一处宋代古船遗址。文兴码头是一平缓的斜坡状台阶，水深较浅，便于低潮位时小船停靠。美山码头的造型为边坡较陡的墩台，便于高潮位时大船停靠。

Jiangkou Wharf

Jiangkou Wharf is the remains of Fashi Port, a once important inner port on the outskirts of Quanzhou. Located southeast of the ancient city of Quanzhou, on the north bank of the Jinjiang River, it was an important location where the exchange of goods between land and sea transport occurred. There remain two piers, at Wenxing and Meishan, and a shipwreck from the Song Dynasty. Wenxing Wharf is a gently descending staircase, built in shallow waters, making it convenient for small boats to dock at low tide. Meishan Wharf is a pier with much steeper steps, making it easier for large ships to dock at high tide.

石湖码头、六胜塔

石湖码头是泉州外港码头，位于石湖半岛西岸，是天然避风良港。石湖码头附近的六胜塔始建于北宋，重建于元代，位于石湖半岛北端的金钗山（又称烟墩山）上，兀立于泉州湾中部，与其东侧大坠岛、小坠岛之间的岱屿门主航道遥遥相对，是进入泉州湾内港的地标。

◎ 六胜塔。（陈英杰 摄）
Liusheng Pagoda. (Photo by Chen Yingjie)

Shihu Dock and Liusheng Pagoda

Shihu Dock is one of Quanzhou's outer wharves, located on the west bank of Shihu Peninsula, and is in a naturally sheltered harbour. Liusheng Pagoda is near Shihu Dock and was originally built in the Northern Song Dynasty, before being rebuilt in the Yuan Dynasty. It is located on Jinchai Mountain, also known as Yandun Mountain, on the northern end of Shihu Peninsula. As this is relatively central along Quanzhou Bay, it is directly opposite Daiyumen Channel between Dazhui Island and Xiaozhui Island into Quanzhou Port, making it a notable landmark.

◎ 石湖码头。（陈英杰 摄）
Shihu Dock. (Photo by Chen Yingjie)

◎ 万寿塔建基于宝盖山顶，塔高虽只有 23 米，登塔远望，商舶往来尽收眼底。（泉州市文物局 供图）

Wanshou Pagoda was built on top of Baogai Mountain. Although only 23 metres tall, it can be seen from afar and boasts a panoramic view of shipping lines. (Courtesy of Quanzhou Municipal Cultural Relics Bureau)

万寿塔

万寿塔，建于南宋绍兴年间，位于泉州城东南的宝盖山。这里控扼泉州湾与外海交界处。又因民间长期流传着姑嫂二人登塔眺望出海者归来的传说，俗称姑嫂塔。宝盖山矗立于泉州湾与深沪湾之间的平原丘陵上，是泉州湾南最高峰。船从南方驶入泉州湾，万寿塔巍然屹立，昼可见塔，夜能见灯，自古便是来船抵达泉州湾的航标。

Wanshou Pagoda

Built between 1131 and 1162 of the Southern Song Dynasty, Wanshou Pagoda is located on Baogai Mountain, southeast from Quanzhou City, offering a commanding view of Quanzhou Bay and the open sea. Local folklore claims that two sisters-in-law climbed the tower to watch the return of loved ones, so the tower is sometimes known as "Gusao Pagoda (Pagoda of the Sisters-in-Law)". Baogai Mountain stands on the plains and hills between Quanzhou Bay and Shenhu Bay, and boasts the highest altitude south of Quanzhou Bay. As Wanshou Pagoda stood tall above, ships sailing into Quanzhou Bay are visible from there both during the day and at night. Since ancient times, it has served as a beacon for ships coming into Quanzhou Bay.

洛阳桥、安平桥

　　泉州港以八闽城乡为腹地依托，有赖于江河与驿道的连通。入宋以后，泉州地区迎来了建造桥梁的高潮，其中以洛阳桥、安平桥和顺济桥最具代表性。

　　洛阳桥于 1059 年落成，打通了泉州北上福州乃至内陆腹地的交通动脉，更因北宋著名书法家、文学家蔡襄主持建造而久负盛名。洛阳桥是中国现存的第一座跨海梁式石桥，也是官方、僧侣和各界商民集资建桥的典范。能工巧匠们首创了"筏形基础""养蛎固基""浮运架梁"等先进技术，为后世造桥积累了宝贵经验。

　　位于泉州城西南的安平桥，则完全改善了刺桐港南下的交通。安平桥始建于 1138 年，历时 14 年告成。桥长约五华里，故俗称五里桥，并因此赢得了"天下无桥长此桥"的美誉。

◎ 洛阳桥，古称万安桥，位于泉州城东北洛阳江入海口，江水与海潮汇合于此。（吴云轩 摄）
Once called Wan'an Bridge, Luoyang Bridge is situated at the mouth of the Luoyang River northeast of Quanzhou City, with river water and sea tides meeting here. (Photo by Wu Yunxuan)

Luoyang Bridge and Anping Bridge

Quanzhou Port relied on the goods of other areas of Fujian for its success, as well as the road and river connections between them. During the Song Dynasty, a large number of bridges were built in Quanzhou, the most iconic being the Luoyang Bridge, Anping Bridge and Shunji Bridge.

Luoyang Bridge was completed in 1059, creating a channel for traffic between Quanzhou and Fuzhou as well as other inland areas. It was made even more famous as Cai Xiang, a well-known calligrapher and writer, led the construction of the bridge. It is China's earliest extant stone sea-crossing bridge and was funded jointly by the government, monks, and merchants. The architects made use of revolutionary technologies such as "raft-shaped foundations" "reinforcing the foundation by cultivating oysters" and "transporting heavy stone slabs by using buoyancy forces and waves", leaving a legacy for future bridge-builders.

Located in southwest Quanzhou City is Anping Bridge, a bridge that created massive improvements for southbound traffic towards Quanzhou. Built in 1138, it took fourteen years to complete the bridge. It is also commonly known as "Wuli Bridge", a reference to its length of five li (one li is approximately half a kilometre) and was sometimes referred to as "the longest bridge with no equal in the world".

◎ 安平桥。（陈英杰 摄）
Anping Bridge. (Photo by Chen Yingjie)

顺济桥遗址、德济门遗址

　　随着泉州城日渐向南发展，古城南门外建起了顺济桥。此桥建于 1211 年，横跨晋江两岸，以近顺济宫（天后宫）而得名，现存船形桥墩及桥墩遗址多处。1230 年前后，泉州城又一次扩大，在顺济桥与天后宫之间建起了南城门德济门。德济门位于全城繁华要地，内通城区，外连海港，成为城南地标。顺济桥遗址与德济门遗址，保存着泉州向南拓建、发展和演变的历史印迹，也见证着刺桐城南商圈的兴衰。

◎ 顺济桥遗址。（陈英杰 摄）
Site of Shunji Bridge. (Photo by Chen Yingjie)

◎ 天后宫前的德济门遗址。（陈英杰 摄）
Site of Deji Gate in front of Tianhou Temple. (Photo by Chen Yingjie)

Site of Shunji Bridge and Site of Deji Gate

As Quanzhou City sprawled southwards, Shunji Bridge was built outside the city walls of the ancient city of Quanzhou. Built in 1211 across the banks of Jinjiang River, it was named after Shunji Temple (Tianhou Temple). There are several remaining boat-shaped piers and pier sites. Around 1230, Quanzhou City expanded once again, and Deji Gate was built between Shunji Bridge and Tianhou Temple. Located in an affluent part of the city, it connected the inner city to the docks on the outer edge, making it a landmark of the south section of Quanzhou City. Site of Shunji Bridge and Site of Deji Gate are historical traces of the expansion of Quanzhou to the south as it developed and have borne witness to the rise and fall of the business district in the southern part of Quanzhou City.

◎ 不同的文化传统在这里交汇，不同的宗教信仰在这里融合。（傅捷雄 摄）

Quanzhou: a melting pot of different cultures and religions. (Photo by Fu Jiexiong)

■ 海滨邹鲁　光明之城

　　自六朝以来，"衣冠南渡，八姓入闽"；到唐五代，陈元光的"开漳"，王潮、王审知的入闽，为闽南一带引来大量中原汉人和中原文化。唐五代以来的福建主政者热衷推行教化，闽人逐渐重视科举，儒家文化广为传播。宋元时代，福建文教兴盛，人才辈出，两宋科举及第者有数万人之多。南宋著名的理学家朱熹，更成为闽学学派的创立者。

　　随着海上丝绸之路的日渐繁荣，商舶所到之地越来越广，中国商人由此启程走向世界，世界各地的商人也纷纷来到泉州。无论是波斯人、阿拉伯人，还是印度人、犹太人，无论是佛教、道教，还是基督教、伊斯兰教、摩尼教等，人们超越了民族和宗教的差异，共处一城。刺桐，孕育出了开放、多元的独特文化，也创造了一个包容互鉴、和谐共存的社会。

福建的文化与自然遗产
Cultural and Natural Heritage in Fujian

■ Land of Culture and Education & City of Light

From the Six Dynasties period to the Five Dynasties and Ten Kingdoms period, there was a large amount of immigration south to Fujian from the Central Plains of China, bringing with it the culture of the Central Plains. A greater emphasis was placed on the importance of education and Confucianism was widely spread in Fujian, with Fujian governors promoting it from the late Tang Dynasty. Tens of thousands of Fujianese looked to take imperial exams during the Song Dynasty. It is during this time in the Song and Yuan dynasties that Fujian's culture and education flourished, and many talented people came into existence. Zhu Xi, a famous Neo-Confucianist in the Southern Song Dynasty, became the founder of the Min School of Confucianism.

With the increasing prosperity of the Maritime Silk Road, Chinese merchants departed for overseas ventures from Quanzhou, and people from all corners of the world came to Quanzhou. Regardless of ethnicity, nationality or religion, people were welcomed into Quanzhou and lived together. This diverse and open culture led to a harmonious coexistence filled with mutual learning.

泉州府文庙

　　文庙，是儒家祭祀场所。泉州府文庙及学宫，既包含儒家祭祀建筑，也囊括了地方教育机构，其布局极为匀称：东侧是学宫，中间是崇圣祠，西侧是文庙。文庙建筑群始建于976年，主体格局形成于1137年，规制完整，气势宏大。文庙反映了泉州人文荟萃、崇儒重文的特点，是宋元时代泉州文教昌盛的结晶。

Quanzhou Confucian Temple and School

A place for Confucian worship, Quanzhou Confucian Temple and School was a complex that began construction in 976, containing both places of worship and educational institutions. Built in a very symmetrical fashion, the west side was dedicated to Confucian sacrifice, the east side to educational facilities and in the middle sits Chongsheng Shrine. The complex's structure did not take form until 1137, with a large scale and complete pattern. The Confucian Temple is a record of Quanzhou's gathering of talented people, advanced culture and its advocating Confucianism and literature, and is the result of Quanzhou's development in education and culture during the Song and Yuan dynasties.

◎ 泉州府文庙。（陈英杰 摄）
Quanzhou Confucian Temple and School. (Photo by Chen Yingjie)

◎ 开元寺大雄宝殿。（陈英杰 摄）
The Mahavira Hall of Kaiyuan Temple. (Photo by Chen Yingjie)

开元寺

　　开元寺创寺于 686 年，位于泉州城内西街，经历代兴扩，到宋元时期盛极一时，至今仍是福建规模最大的佛教寺院。寺内最著名的东西塔为南宋时重建，是中国最高的一对石塔，塔身装饰的 160 尊浮雕，多数是印度神话和佛教故事中的人物，却在中国工匠的造像中表现出汉人面目和气质。大雄宝殿前月台的须弥座上，饰有印度教狮身人面像石雕，殿内斗拱饰 24 尊妙音鸟式飞天乐伎，殿后檐明间两柱为辉绿岩雕刻的印度教石柱。这种融合，呈现出中外文化深度交融、宗教艺术发达繁荣的景象。

◎ 斗拱上的飞天乐伎。（陈英杰 摄）
The flying fairies with instruments on the bracket sets. (Photo by Chen Yingjie)

Kaiyuan Temple

Built in 686, Kaiyuan Temple sits in the West Street of Quanzhou. The temple was expanded in the subsequent Song and Yuan dynasties and is the largest Buddhist temple in Fujian. The East Pagoda and West Pagoda are its most famous features, being the tallest pair of stone pagodas in China, and were rebuilt during the Southern Song Dynasty. There are 160 relief sculptures on the pagodas, most of which are figures from Indian mythology and Buddist stories. These sulptures exhibit the features and temperament of Han people after the Chinese craftsmen engraved them. The Sumeru pedestal facade on the front platform is inlaid with Hindu Sphinx relief figures and inside the Mahavira Hall are 24 carved flying Asparas resembling Kalavinka. The two pillars at the very rear of the hall are Hindu stone pillars carved out of diabase. Kaiyuan Temple is a prime example of the fusion of Chinese and foreign cultures, as well as their religions.

老君岩造像

　　清源山南麓的老君岩造像，以一块天然巨石雕凿而成。这座老子巨型石雕像，具有明显的尊重自然、亲近自然的道教建筑手笔。老君席地而坐，双腿盘屈，体态安闲。这样工程浩大的石雕造像完成于宋代，体现了当时泉州道教的兴盛和雄厚的经济实力。

Statue of Lao Tze

The statue of Lao Tze at the foothills of Mount Qingyuan is carved out of a massive natural rock. The giant statue of Lao Tze is clearly reverent of the nature around him, holding true to Taoist values. He is depicted in a benevolent, resting manner with crossed legs. The stone sculpture was completed during the Song Dynasty, reflecting the prosperity of Taoism and the abundant economic power of Quanzhou at the time.

◎ 清源山老君岩高 5.63 米，宽 8.01 米，由一整块石头雕凿而成。（吴刚强 摄）
Carved from a single massive rock, the statue of Lao Tze is 5.63m tall, 8.01m wide and sits at the foothills of Mount Qingyuan. (Photo by Wu Gangqiang)

伊斯兰教圣墓

　　泉州作为国际性的贸易大港，阿拉伯客商接踵而来，伊斯兰教随之传入。据记载，唐代来中国传教的穆罕默德的两大门徒去世后葬在泉州东郊的灵山，人称"圣墓"。

Islamic Tombs

As an international trading port, Quanzhou attracted many Arabic traders, who brought with them the Islamic religion. According to historic records, two disciples of Muhammad came to China to preach in the Tang Dynasty. They were buried after death at the southern foothills of Lingshan Mountain, and the location is now referred to as the Islamic Tombs.

◎ 伊斯兰教圣墓。（陈英杰 摄）
Islamic Tombs. (Photo by Chen Yingjie)

清净寺

阿拉伯客商的聚居地在古城南墙外，距商业区很近，伊斯兰教信徒在此建造了清净寺，便于开展宗教礼拜活动。清净寺（又名圣友寺），建于北宋大中祥符二年（1009），并在穆斯林主导下多次修缮。寺院整体为伊斯兰建筑风格，现存门楼、礼拜堂、明善堂等建筑以及多方与寺院历史有关的碑刻。

Qingjing Mosque

The Arabic merchant quarter was located just outside of the south city wall of Quanzhou, not far from the commercial centre of the city. Muslims built Qingjing Mosque here in order to facilitate worship and prayers. Qingjing Mosque, also known as Shengyou Mosque, was built in 1009 during the Northern Song Dynasty, and has undergone multiple repairs under Muslim leadership. The mosque is of typical Islamic architecture, and remaining structures include the arch gate, Prayer Hall, Mingshan Hall and several inscribed steles connected to the history of the mosque.

◎ 夕阳与灯火辉映下的清净寺。（陈英杰 摄）
The Qingjing Mosque illuminated by the setting sun and the lights. (Photo by Chen Yingjie)

草庵摩尼光佛石像

　　唐代，摩尼教随波斯商人的足迹，经陆路从西域来到中国，传入泉州。在长期的演变过程中，摩尼教吸收佛教、道教的思想，并逐渐演化为明教。摩尼教最重要的史迹，是位于泉州城南华表山东麓的草庵。草庵始建于宋，最初为草构，到元代改为石构，依山而筑，称草庵寺。

Statue of Mani in Cao'an Temple

During the Tang Dynasty, Persian merchants brought Manichaeism to China overland from the Western Regions, spreading their religion in Quanzhou. Over the course of time, this branch of Manichaeism absorbed ideas from Buddhism and Taoism, gradually becoming "Minjiao", the religion of light. As the most important monument of Manichaeism, Cao'an Temple is located at the eastern foot of Huabiao Hill, south of Quanzhou City. Originally built as a straw building in the Song Dynasty, it was replaced by a stone building during the Yuan Dynasty, but retained *cao* (straw) in its name, Cao'an Temple.

◎ 草庵摩尼光佛石像雕凿于 1339 年，是世界现存唯一的摩尼光佛造像。（何国辉 摄）
The statue of Mani in Cao'an Temple was carved in 1339, and is the only one of its kind in the world. (Photo by He Guohui)

三坊七巷
Three Lanes and Seven Alleys

遗产价值

　　福州三坊七巷是一处延续了上千年的城市住区，其街巷格局是中国传统坊巷制度的延续与发展，保存完好的街区形态是中国古代城市住区肌理和城市景观的突出例证。这片源于里坊制度的城市居住空间也是历代士人阶层聚居生活的场所，生动地展现出这一阶层的生活状态，清晰地表达出这一阶层共有的家国理想和个体对道德修养的追求，以及他们对其他阶层的强烈影响。从宅园到坊巷再到街区，乃至与整个城市的关联关系，三坊七巷清晰的空间层次与组织关系映射出中国历代封建王朝延续的严谨、统一的社会秩序，成为中国古代儒家所倡导的"修齐治平"伦理哲学和政治理论的独特反映。

◎ 三坊七巷全景。（林武旺 摄）
A panoramic view of Three Lanes and Seven Alleys. (Photo by Lin Wuwang)

Universal Value

Three·Lanes and Seven Alleys of Fuzhou is an urban residential area existing for more than a thousand years. Its street pattern is a continuum of the traditional Lane System (an urban planning system evolved from Lifang System), while the well-preserved spatial structure represents an outstanding example of the urban fabric and cityscape of a residential area in ancient China. Having evolved from the Lifang System, this urban area is also a place where the literati and officialdom class chose to live in the past dynasties. It vividly illustrates the living conditions of this class, and clearly expresses their common idea and value on the state and family, their individual pursuit of moral integrity and self-cultivation, and their intense and profound impact on other classes of the society. The associative relationship between individual houses, the lanes and alleys, the whole area of the nominated property, and the entire city are articulated with clear spatial layers and a well-organized structure, which reflects the rigorous and unified social order that existed in the past feudal dynasties as a unique manifestation of the ethical philosophy and political theory of "cultivating one's morality, regulating the family, managing the country and harmonizing the world" held in esteem by the Confucians in ancient China.

三坊七巷自晋代初现，因其特殊的地理位置和历史文化积淀，逐渐成为中国古代士人阶层聚集的生活空间，清至民国走向繁盛。三坊七巷整个街区和内部的众多宅园，系统地保留着这一阶层在清朝末年退出历史舞台之际的群体生活环境。从个体的生活场所，到承载家族的宅园，再到坊巷中的邻里，乃至整个坊巷社区和其外部环境，处处展现出这一群体在精神文化方面普遍的高雅追求，同时又在各个层次上呈现出清晰、严谨的空间秩序和统一格调。这些又深刻地影响到街区中的其他阶层，从而发展成整个片区的整体风貌特色和突出品质，使这里成为世人向往的生活场所。因此，以儒家文化为根基的士人阶层历经千年所形成的"修身，齐家，治国，平天下"这一封建伦理政治哲学体系，在三坊七巷这一历史悠久的城市住区得以实践和见证。

◎ 三坊七巷中颇具代表性的私家宅园小黄楼，建筑格局精巧，花园移步换景。（俞松 摄）
Xiaohuanglou, a representative private residence in Three Lanes and Seven Alleys, with an exemplary garden and exquisite architecture. (Photo by Yu Song)

◎ 坊巷夜色。（林武旺 摄）

Alleys by night. (Photo by Lin Wuwang)

Because of the unique geographic location and its history and culture, the site, first built during the Jin Dynasty (3rd—4th century CE), reached its peak during the Qing Dynasty and Republican period (1636—1949), and had gradually become living quarters where the ancient Chinese literati and officialdom class gathered. The whole area and the various houses and gardens within it exhibit the living conditions of the class as they were when it stepped down the stage of history at the end of the Qing Dynasty. Every place, from the individual living places to the houses and gardens once belonging to those clans, to the lanes and alleys of the whole area and their surroundings, exhibits the common high spiritual and cultural pursuits of the class, and at the same time clearly represents a strict layered spatial order and unity of the place. All these features had a profound influence on other classes of the society living in the area, thus resulted in the distinct style and the outstanding quality of the area, making it an ideal living place for people in the past. Therefore, as a historical urban residential area, Three Lanes and Seven Alleys is an outstanding testimony of how the class of literati and officialdom, who held beliefs deeply rooted in Confucianism, had practiced the Chinese feudal ethical philosophy and political theory of "cultivating one's morality, regulating the family, managing the country and harmonizing the world" for over a thousand years.

◎ 严谨清晰的坊巷格局。（颜家蔚 摄）

The ordered pattern of lanes and alleys, as seen from above. (Photo by Yan Jiawei)

　　三坊七巷保存着延续了上千年的街巷格局，其地上遗存与地下遗址共同反映出福州古城自唐宋以来城市格局由里坊制到坊巷制的变迁和发展。其与城市总体格局的紧密联系，组织严谨的坊巷格局，清晰完整的街巷结构单元和均匀排布其中、形制统一却内涵各异的宅园建筑，以及铭刻在文儒坊内的管理制度，共同成为中国古代城市住区肌理、城市景观特征以及城市住区组织管理模式的突出例证。

Three Lanes and Seven Alleys preserves a street pattern that has lasted for more than a thousand years, while the relics above and under the ground reflect the evolution of the urban structure of ancient Fuzhou City from the Lifang System to the Lane System since the Tang and the Song dynasties. The close connection between this area and the overall layout of the city, the strictly planned street pattern with evenly distributed blocks, the unified form of the houses but with diverse courtyards and private gardens, the carefully selected materials and well-constructed buildings, and the traditional community management system with its rules engraved on a stele in Wenru Lane, altogether represent an outstanding example of the urban fabric in the residential area, the features of the cityscape, and the organization and management model of the residential area in ancient Chinese cities.

◎ 郎官巷。（俞松 摄）
Langguan Alley. (Photo by Yu Song)

◎ 塔巷。（俞松 摄）
Taxiang Alley. (Photo by Yu Song)

◎ 三坊七巷中轴线——南后街。（颜家蔚 摄）

Nanhou Street, the central axis of Three Lanes and Seven Alleys. (Photo by Yan Jiawei)

三坊七巷漫步

　　三坊七巷位于福州市鼓楼区八一七北路西侧，以南后街为轴线，三坊在西，七巷在东，坊巷均为东西走向。自北向南三坊为衣锦坊、文儒坊、光禄坊，七巷为杨桥巷、郎官巷、塔巷、黄巷、安民巷、宫巷、吉庇巷。三坊七巷西侧的文儒坊西段遗址，通过晚唐、宋和明、清等各个时代的地层遗迹，揭示出现今的道路格局与唐宋坊巷格局间清晰的承接对应关系，显示了坊巷与唐宋福州古城的明显联系，见证了三坊七巷上千年的悠久历史和中国古代里坊制度的变迁历程。

◎ 衣锦坊游趣。（林武旺 摄）
Wandering around Yijin Lane. (Photo by Lin Wuwang)

◎ 宫巷绿荫。（林武旺 摄）
The green shade of Gongxiang Alley. (Photo by Lin Wuwang)

A Stroll around Three Lanes and Seven Alleys

Three Lanes and Seven Alleys is located on the west side of Bayiqi North Road, Gulou District, Fuzhou. With Nanhou Street as a reference point, the three lanes are to the west, and the seven alleys to the east, each one running east-west. From north to south, the three lanes refer to Yijin Lane, Wenru Lane and Guanglu Lane; the seven alleys refer to Yangqiao Alley, Langguan Alley, Taxiang Alley, Huangxiang Alley, Anmin Alley, Gongxiang Alley and Jipi Alley. Stratigraphic studies applied to Wenru Lane have demonstrated clear links from the late Tang Dynasty through to the Qing dynasty, and the current organization of roads is a reflection of the Tang and Song dynasties' systems, providing evidence that Three Lanes and Seven Alleys is a remnant of the ancient city of Fuzhou, having withstood the test of time, and the result of the evolution of the Lifang System in ancient China.

◎ 二梅书屋因院内种植有两棵梅花树而得名。（俞松 摄）
Ermei Study is named after the two plum trees planted in its courtyard. (Photo by Yu Song)

这一处面积不大、步行即可游览的历史街区，自唐以来，走出过数百位历史名人，包括政治家、军事家、文学家，黄璞、陈烈、张经、甘国宝、沈葆桢、严复、林旭、林觉民、冰心、郁达夫等都曾居住于此。坊巷之中至今仍保存着大量明、清时期的民居建筑和庭院园林，呈现出粉墙黛瓦、深宅大院、石板小巷的原始风貌。典型代表有林觉民故居、水榭戏台、欧阳氏民居、陈承裘故居、严复故居、二梅书屋、小黄楼、林氏民居、沈葆桢故居等。

A small historical district, Three Lanes and Seven Alleys can easily be visited on foot. Since the Tang Dynasty, hundreds of notable people have lived here, including statesmen, military commanders, scholars—Huang Pu, Chen Lie, Zhang Jing, Gan Guobao, Shen Baozhen, Yan Fu, Lin Xu, Lin Juemin, Bing Xin, Yu Dafu, just to name a few. Even today, a number of residential buildings and courtyards remain from the Ming and Qing dynasties, with white walls, large courtyards and flagstone paths. Some typical examples are Lin Juemin's Former Residence, the Waterside Stage, Ouyang Family Residence, Chen Chengqiu's Former Residence, Yan Fu's Former Residence, Ermei Study, Xiaohuanglou, Lin Family Residence and Shen Baozhen's Former Residence.

◎ 粉墙黛瓦的三坊七巷被誉为"中国明清古建筑博物馆"。（李芳 摄）

With white walls and black roof-tiles, Three Lanes and Seven Alleys has been described as China's "Museum of Ancient Ming and Qing Architecture". (Photo by Li Fang)

◎ 林觉民故居，中国现代著名作家冰心也曾在此居住过。（林武旺 摄）

Lin Juemin's Former Residence, also where the famous modern Chinese writer Bing Xin once lived. (Photo by Lin Wuwang)

■ 林觉民故居

　　林觉民是中国近代著名的革命烈士，他就义前所留下的绝笔《与妻书》至今仍广受中国青年的喜爱。其故居位于南后街西侧北口与杨桥路交会处，坐西向东，为清式木构建筑。

■ Lin Juemin's Former Residence

Lin Juemin is a famous revolutionary martyr of modern China. His *Letter of Farewell to My Wife*, written days before his death, is considered a literary masterpiece, popular among young people even today. His former residence is a wooden building of Qing Dynasty style, facing east, located where the western side of Nanhou Street meets Yangqiao Road.

■ 水榭戏台

　　水榭戏台所在民居位于衣锦坊东口北侧，创建于明万历间（1573—1620），后经多次改建，清道光年间（1821—1850）建成三座毗连、全坊最大的宅院。戏台位于水池之上、假山之侧，是福州唯一建于民居里的戏台，至今仍然可以使用，偶有闽剧名角登台表演，伴着园中青翠草木、池里欢快锦鲤，带给观众近在咫尺却恍若穿越千年的独特感受。

■ The Waterside Theatre

The Waterside Theatre is found in a residence to the north of the east entrance of Yijin Lane. Built between 1573 and 1620 in the Ming Dynasty, it was reconstructed a number of times before its current form of three adjacent buildings was completed between 1821 and 1850 during the Qing Dynasty. The stage of this biggest residence in Yijin Lane is perched above a pool of water and beside the rockery for a better viewing experience. It is the only theatrical stage built in a residential building in Fuzhou and is still in use today. Occasionally, famous Fujian Opera singers will grace the stage; and combined with the green vegetation and playful koi in the pool, the scene can take the audience back hundreds of years to a different time.

◎ 衣锦坊水榭戏台。（黄恒日 摄）
The Waterside Theatre in Yijin Lane. (Photo by Huang Hengri)

◎ 欧阳氏民居。（林振寿 摄）
Ouyang Family Residence. (Photo by Lin Zhenshou)

■ 欧阳氏民居

　　欧阳氏民居位于衣锦坊中段南侧，据族谱记载，该建筑始建于清乾隆年间（1736—1796），清光绪十六年（1890）由福州商界传奇人物欧阳氏兄弟重修。其中，坐落在首进院落西侧的欧阳花厅为整座宅院的精华，有着大、奇、精、巧等特色。

■ Ouyang Family Residence

Ouyang Family Residence is located to the south of Yijin Lane's middle section. According to genealogical records, the building was first built between 1736 and 1796 during the Qing Dynasty, but was rebuilt by the Ouyang brothers, famed Fuzhou merchants, in 1890. Ouyang Parlour, located to the west of the first courtyard, is the cherry on top of this ancient residence—spacious, fancy, sophisticated, and completely ingenious.

◎ 陈承裘故居。（林武旺 摄）

Chen Chengqiu's Former Residence. (Photo by Lin Wuwang)

■ 陈承裘故居

　　陈承裘故居位于文儒坊偏西处的南面，为清代建筑，是清末帝师陈宝琛之父陈承裘的宅邸，因建筑构件用料考究、精雕细刻而闻名。陈承裘六个儿子都登科及第，成为民间佳话，故有"六子科甲"的横匾高悬于门额之上。

■ Chen Chengqiu's Former Residence

The former residence of Chen Chengqiu is located in the southwest of Wenru Lane, built in the Qing Dynasty. Chen Chengqiu was the father of Chen Baochen, a trusted advisor of the last emperor in Chinese history. The residence itself is famous for its valuable materials and meticulous carvings. All the six of Chen Chengqiu's sons passed the imperial examination, a feat commemorated by a plaque engraved with "Liu Zi Ke Jia" above the gate.

◎ 严复故居。（林振寿 摄）

Yan Fu's Former Residence. (Photo by Lin Zhenshou)

■ 严复故居

　　作为中国近代极具影响力的资产阶级启蒙思想家和著名的翻译家、教育家，严复被誉为中国近代史上向西方国家寻找真理的"先进的中国人"之一。其故居位于郎官巷西段，坐北向南，主座与花厅相邻。花厅是严复晚年居住的地方，他在这里写下了近百篇诗词和信札。

■ Yan Fu's Former Residence

A highly influential philosopher, scholar and translator in modern China, Yan Fu is known as one of the "advanced Chinese" who sought to introduce western ideas to China. His former residence is located in the west section of Langguan Alley, facing south. The main building is located next to the parlour, where he lived in his later years and wrote nearly a hundred poems and letters.

■ 二梅书屋

二梅书屋位于郎官巷西段南侧，为清代著名地方志专家和教育家林星章的住宅，始建于明末，清光绪（1875—1908）及民国（1912—1949）年间重修。书屋各院落之间有围墙相隔，墙头灰塑、彩绘纹饰工艺精美，花厅为其精华所在，厅前小花园中还有一株百年古荔枝树，依旧春华秋实。

■ Ermei Study

Ermei Study is in the southwestern section of Langguan Alley. It was the home of Lin Xingzhang, a well-known expert in chorography and educator during the Qing Dynasty. Initially built towards the end of the Ming Dynasty, the study has been reconstructed many times between 1875 and 1949. The main buildings are separated by stone walls, on which exquisite patterns and sculptures are displayed. The parlour is equally impressive, and just outside of it is a century-old lychee tree which still bears fruit.

◎ 二梅书屋花园。（叶诚 摄）
The garden of Ermei Study. (Photo by Ye Cheng)

■ 小黄楼

　　小黄楼位于黄巷，唐代鸿儒、文阁校书郎黄璞曾在此居住，现存建筑为清代学者梁章钜所建。小黄楼建筑群与楼前假山、水池、石桥、半边亭相得益彰，是典型的由建筑、山水、花木等组合而成的闹中取静、小中见大的城市山水庭院。

■ Xiaohuanglou

Xiaohuanglou is found in Huangxiang Alley, where the Tang Dynasty learned scholar Huang Pu once lived. The extant building was built by Liang Zhangju, a scholar of the Qing Dynasty. The buildings, the pond, the stone bridge and the pavilion in Xiaohuanglou complement each other, which shows the scene of a typical Chinese courtyard, designed to pursue quietness in a noisy neighbourhood and create an immersive experience in a small space—a manifestation of much in little.

◎ 布局精巧的小黄楼。（林振寿 摄）
The meticulous design of Xiaohuanglou's landscaping. (Photo by Lin Zhenshou)

■ 林氏民居

　　林氏民居位于宫巷，这里曾为南明王朝（1644—1662）的大理寺衙门，后为"中国开眼看世界的第一人"林则徐之次子林聪彝所居。民居由主座及其东侧的两个跨院组成，跨院在中部围出大片的空地作为园林，花厅的建筑构件显示了当时福州工匠的高超技艺。

■ Lin Family Residence

Lin Family Residence is located in Gongxiang Alley, once the location of a Dalisi yamen (the supreme judicial organization of ancient times) during the Nanming Dynasty (1644—1662), and later the residence for the second son of Lin Zexu, a prominent scholar-official of the Qing Dynasty who was honoured as "the first Chinese to open eyes to observe the world" and had a large impact on the Opium War. The residence is made up of three buildings surrounding a large courtyard that serves as a garden. The architectural components of the parlour are a demonstration of the extraordinary skill of Fuzhou craftsmen at the time.

◎ 林氏民居庭院。（俞松 摄）
The courtyard of Lin Family Residence. (Photo by Yu Song)

■ 沈葆桢故居

　　沈葆桢是晚清时期的重要政治家、军事家、外交家，是中国近代造船、航运、海军建设事业的奠基人之一。其故居位于宫巷，为明、清典型民居，坐北向南，周围有封火墙，建筑中轴线自南而北，依次为门头房、厅堂、正座、藏书楼。

■ Shen Baozhen's Former Residence

Shen Baozhen was an important official, military strategist and diplomat in the late Qing Dynasty. He was also one of the founders of modern Chinese shipbuilding, shipping and navy. His former residence is located in Gongxiang Alley and is of a style typical of the Ming and Qing dynasties. Facing south, it is surrounded by firewalls and there are the gatehouse, the hall, the main building and the library building, centred on a south-north axis.

◎ 沈葆桢故居。（林振寿 摄）
Shen Baozhen's Former Residence. (Photo by Lin Zhenshou)

海上丝绸之路（中国福建段）
The Maritime Silk Road (Fujian Section in China)

◎ 始建于北宋皇祐五年（1053）的洛阳桥为中国第一座跨海梁式大石桥，位于古泉州湾洛阳港，是海外贸易兴盛的见证。（王胜 摄）

First constructed in 1053 during the Northern Song Dynasty, Luoyang Bridge is China's first sea-crossing stone girder bridge. It is located at Luoyang Port, Quanzhou Bay, and speaks volumes for the prosperity of international trade. (Photo by Wang Sheng)

遗产价值

　　海上丝绸之路始于公元前 2 世纪的西汉年间，兴于公元 8 世纪的唐代中叶，盛于公元 10 至 14 世纪的宋、元时期，至 17 世纪的明代后期逐渐衰落。海上丝绸之路的交通网络分布于中国跨海向东至朝鲜半岛、日本，向南向西绵延至印度洋、阿拉伯海、地中海沿岸各国。在此近两千年中，亚洲、非洲、欧洲沿海各国家和民族通过海上丝绸之路进行的政治交往、贸易往来、文化交流、宗教传播、技术交流、民族迁徙、物产交流等全方位的人类活动，对世界文明发展进程产生了巨大影响。海上丝绸之路为人类文明和文化发展及共同繁荣做出了重要贡献。

　　福建段海上丝绸之路历史悠久，积淀丰厚，文化遗迹众多。有福州的怀安窑址、恩赐琅琊郡王德政碑、邢港码头（迴龙桥）；东方第一大港泉州港的万寿塔、六胜塔、石湖码头、江口码头；见证泉州官方主导对外贸易的市舶司遗址、南外宗正司遗址、德济门遗址、九日山祈风石刻；见证对外贸易交通繁荣的洛阳桥、安平桥和顺济桥遗址；热销世界的福建制造和交通运输遗址有磁灶窑、闽清义窑、德化窑、安溪青阳下草埔冶铁遗址、海坛海峡水下遗址、连江定海水下遗址、南胜窑、东溪窑、土坑村港市；充分显示泉州多元文化交融的开元寺、伊斯兰教圣墓、清净寺、草庵摩尼光佛造像、泉州府文庙、真武庙、清源山老君岩造像、湄洲妈祖庙、泉州天后宫、世家坑；与郑和下西洋相关的圣寿宝塔及天妃灵应记碑、登文道码头、罗星塔；与"海禁"有关的漳州月港的古街古迹等等。

◎ 位于古泉州港南郊石狮市蚶江镇石湖村半岛上的石湖码头，相传最早为唐开元年间（713 — 741）航海家林銮创建。北宋熙宁元年（1068）建水寨以作军事上的防御之用，北宋元祐年间（1086 — 1094），侍禁傅琎在码头左侧创建"通济栈桥"，成为一个颇具特色的"顺岸码头"，是 11—14 世纪泉州港水水转运和水陆转运的重要码头。（陈起拓 摄）

Shihu Wharf, located on the peninsula of Shihu Village of Shishi City, is said to have been founded by the navigator Lin Luan during 713-741 in the Tang Dynasty. In 1068, a military fort was constructed on the coast. During the Northern Song Dynasty (1086-1094), Fu Jin built "Tongji Wharf", which later became the distinctive Shun'an Wharf, a key wharf for the exchange of transported goods in Quanzhou Port from the 11th to 14th centuries. (Photo by Chen Qituo)

Universal Value

The Maritime Silk Road began around 200BCE, during the Western Han Dynasty. It flourished during the 8th century in the Tang Dynasty, all the way through the Song and Yuan dynasties and reached its peak between the 10th and 14th centuries, before gradually declining in the late Ming Dynasty, in the 17th century. The network created by the Maritime Silk Road stretched from China to the Korean peninsula and Japan in the east, and across the Indian Ocean in the south, Arabian Sea to the Mediterranean countries in the west. During the 2,000 years that the Maritime Silk Road was in use, the coastal nations in Asia, Africa and Europe were able to exchange culture, religion, technology, and commerce. It would not be an overstatement to say that the Maritime Silk Road contributed greatly to the development and prosperity of human civilization around the world.

Fujian has had a long history of contributing to the Maritime Silk Road, and as a result, contains many objects and places of cultural significance, including in Fuzhou the Huaian Kiln Site, the stele commemorating the merit of Langya King, Xinggang Wharf and Jionglong Bridge; and the sites of Wanshou Pagoda, Liusheng Pagoda, Shihu Wharf and Jiangkou Wharf, located at Quanzhou Port, the largest port in the East during the peak of the Maritime Silk Road. In addition to these, once officially presiding over international trade routes, there exist the sites of the Maritime Trade Office, Southern Clan Office and the Deji Gate, as well as Jiuri Mountain Wind-Praying Inscriptions. Luoyang Bridge, Anping Bridge and Shunji Bridge have borne witness to the prosperous trade. Related to the various exports out of Fujian are Cizao Kiln, Minqing Yi Kiln, Dehua Kiln, Xiacaopu Iron Production Site of Qingyang Village in Anxi, Haitan Strait Underwater Site, Lianjiang Dinghai Underwater Site, Nansheng Kiln, Dongxi Kiln and Tukeng Village Port. Evidence of the multiculturalism and religious diversity that the Maritime Silk Road brought can be seen at Kaiyuan Temple, the Islamic Tombs, Qingjing Mosque, Statue of Mani in Cao'an Temple, Quanzhou Confucius Temple, Zhenwu Temple, Statue of Lao Tze at Mount Qingyuan, Meizhou Mazu Temple, Tianhou Temple, and Ceylon Prince's family cemetery. Evidence of Zheng He's seven voyages to the West can be found at Shengshou Pagoda, Mazu's Memorial Tablet, Dengwendao Wharf, and Luoxing Pagoda; and Zhangzhou Yuegang historic villages remind us the development of Maritime Silk Road at its end.

海上丝路寻迹

　　丰富的海洋国土资源和河口港湾资源，绵长辽阔的海岸线，优良的港口和季风、洋流，以及内陆交通的便捷和广阔的经济腹地，使福建成为古代中国乃至整个东亚片区沿海上丝绸之路对外货物贸易与人员交流最为繁盛的区域，也是中华海洋文化最重要的发源地。

　　在长达 2,000 多年的历史长河中，这里的先民开展海洋经济和海上贸易，给当地居民带来了巨大利益，促使越来越多的人跻身于海外贸易的大潮中，商贾人士也由此成为当地一个特殊阶层受到尊重，使得这一地区形成了重视商贸的传统。这种传统和海洋经济的发展使东南沿海地区的经济、社会、文化、习俗、信仰等领域都带有明显的海洋性特征。

　　另一方面，海洋环境的凶险也使得人类在向海洋发展与开拓的过程中，出于对超自然与超社会力量的敬畏，诞生了海神信仰，而海上贸易的发展与兴盛，又进一步促进了海神信仰及由此衍生的海神祭祀活动的发展。

Development of the Maritime Silk Road

Boasting abundant marine resources, long, wide coastlines, and favourable currents, Fujian was the perfect place to settle ports and harbours, even before considering its convenient transportation inland. Before long, Fujian became a hub for commercial and cultural exchanges not just in China, but the wider East Asian region, and cemented its place in history as the most important place of China's marine culture.

Over the course of more than 2,000 years, the settlers of Fujian benefited greatly from the development of maritime trade, and merchants became a highly respected class in society. Even now, the culture of Fujian is one which respects entrepreneurship and commerce. Fujian's society, customs, economics and religion have all been impacted by its coastal location.

On the other hand, the dangers of living near the sea have also had an impact on society. There is great respect for the supernatural forces which affect their seafaring lives, such as deities of the sea, and many traditional rituals or sacrifices are derived from this, which became even more important as marine trade developed.

◎ 传说宋建隆元年（960），渔家姑娘林默在莆田湄洲岛出生。她聪明勤学，钻研医道，常帮人防疫治病；她仁慈善良，乐善好施，勇敢坚强。28 岁那年，为救助海难而捐躯大海，"羽化升天"。乡民褒称其"妈祖"，为她在莆田湄洲岛修建了世界上第一座妈祖庙，并称之为"祖庙"。先由福建船民开始，在船上供牌位，奉香火，很快在沿海传开，妈祖成为船民们一致认同的海神。（徐国荣 摄）

Over one thousand years ago in 960 AD, Lin Mo was born into a fisherman's family on Meizhou Island. She studied medicine to help her fellow townspeople prevent and cure diseases. Soon she became known for her kindness and benevolence as well as courage and strong will. At the age of 28, she died attempting to rescue the survivors of a shipwreck, stepped upon a cloud and soared into the heaven. Local residents built a temple in her honour, which became the "ancestral temple". Mazu worship started from fishermen in Fujian, who housed memorial tablets and burned incense in their boats and ships to worship her and the practice soon spread in coastal areas. Mazu has since been venerated as a Goddess of the Sea. (Photo by Xu Guorong)

◎ 九日山祈风石刻位于南安市丰州镇旭山村，是 12 — 13 世纪泉州地方政府主持航海祭祀活动的石刻文字记录，也是现存唯一的古代政府有关航海的国家祭典的石刻文字记录。九日山共有石刻 78 方，其中最珍贵的是刻于南宋淳熙元年（1174）至咸淳二年（1266）的 10 方。祈风石刻体现了古代泉州海上贸易的繁盛及海洋贸易管理制度的成熟，也反映了顺应自然、独具特色的东方海洋文化。（泉州市文物局供图）

Found in Xushan Village, Nan'an City, the Jiuri Mountain Wind-Praying Inscriptions are a record of the worshiping activities hosted by the Quanzhou local government in the 12th and 13th centuries. This is the only stone inscription record of government officiated national ceremonies related to maritime navigation. There are a total of 78 inscriptions, of which the most important are ten stone carvings from 1174 to 1266 of the Southern Song Dynasty. The stone inscriptions are a testament to the prosperity of maritime trade, the maturity of its management system and the unique marine culture that ties humanity to nature. (Courtesy of Quanzhou Municipal Cultural Relics Bureau)

◎ 泉州天后宫位于泉州市鲤城区天后路，建于南宋庆元二年（1196），占地7,200多平方米。大殿供奉天后圣像，殿内保存有清代《勅封天上圣母图》大型壁画。寝殿位于正殿之后。泉州天后宫是中国现存年代最久、规模最大、规格最高的妈祖宫庙。其建筑艺术高超，是海内外众多天后庙宇的建筑范本，也是历史上妈祖信仰重要的传播中心。（泉州市文物局供图）

Tianhou Temple, located on Tianhou Road, Quanzhou City, was built in 1196 during the Southern Song Dynasty and covers over 7,200 square metres. The main hall is dedicated to goddess Mazu and contains a large Qing Dynasty mural dedicated to her. Quanzhou Tianhou Temple is the largest, oldest and most elaborate Mazu temple in China. Its architecture is outstanding, and is the model for many other temples in China and abroad, and the temple itself has been a key location for spreading the beliefs of worshiping Mazu. (Courtesy of Quanzhou Municipal Cultural Relics Bureau)

■ 闽中隆兴

　　福建海上丝绸之路的历史颇为久远。汉元封元年（前110）设东冶县（县治在福州），置东冶港，一时成为东南海运的枢纽和对外贸易的主要港口，海运货物远销日本、夷洲（今台湾）、澶州（今菲律宾），并与中南半岛开辟了定期航线。三国时期，孙吴政权在福州置"典船校尉"，专司造船，又在长溪设"温麻船屯"。唐中叶以后，陆上丝绸之路受阻。至开元年间，在福建设五州，置福建经略使统领。这一时期福建的海上交通与贸易有进一步的发展，福州等港口承担着与外界的交往，福州成为海上丝绸之路的重要港口城市。

■ The Pride of Fujian

The history of Fujian's involvement with the Maritime Silk Road is a long one. In the year 110 BCE, Dongye Port was established in Dongye County, eventually becoming the hub for maritime trade. Trade routes to Japan, the Indochina peninsula, Chanzhou (present-day Philippines), and Yizhou (present-day Taiwan) were established; and to make use of the opportunity presented, the Kingdom of Wu of the Three Kingdoms Period set up ship building academies in Fuzhou and Changxi. As the Tang Dynasty progressed, difficulties were met along the land-based Silk Road. From 713 to 741 during the Tang Dynasty, Fujian as we know it today had been designated as five different states, with Fuzhou being the centre of government. The responsibilities that Fujian undertook as a hub for international trade were stepped up drastically, and Fuzhou became an incredibly important port city that offered access to the Maritime Silk Road.

◎ 怀安窑位于福州市仓山区淮安村。窑址分布面积达 8 万多平方米，有两个厚 1—3 米的文化层堆积，分别为南朝和唐代堆积层。出土南朝器物 3,000 余件，包括钵、盘、杯、碗、茶盏、盘、壶、罐等日常生活用具和多足砚等文具。该窑址所烧造的瓷器大量外销日本等地，在日本鸿胪馆遗址和沉船中均有发现，见证了福州海上丝绸之路贸易的兴盛，是研究南朝至唐五代福建陶瓷烧造技术及其陶瓷外销的重要资料。（福州市文物局供图）

Huaian Kiln is located in Huaian Village, Cangshan District, Fuzhou City. The kiln site covers more than eight hectares, containing two deposits of artifacts, one from the Southern Dynasty and another from the Tang Dynasty. Over 3,000 artifacts from the Southern Dynasty were unearthed, including pots, plates, cups, bowls, teacups, urns, stationery such as inkstones, and other daily utensils. A large number of porcelain pieces were exported to Japan and abroad, having been found in the Japanese ruins of Hongluguan and shipwrecks. A witness to the prosperity of Fuzhou's Maritime Silk Road trade, the kiln site provides important materials for studying the ceramic firing technologies of Japan from the Southern Dynasty through the Tang Dynasty to the Five Dynasties and Ten Kingdoms Period. (Courtesy of Fuzhou Municipal Cultural Relics Bureau)

唐末五代（907–960）王审知及其后裔治闽期间，积极招徕海中"蛮夷商贾"以资公用，并不断将海外商贸所得遣使泛海向中原朝廷进贡，盛况空前。王潮在闽安镇设税课司衙门，负责来往对外贸易船只的课税业务；王审知设"榷货务"专司舶货的征榷事宜，进一步规范了海上贸易的有序进行。公元9到10世纪的福州，不仅向中原王朝进贡精美的纺织品，还将丝绸、茶叶、印刷纸、瓷器等外销至朝鲜半岛、日本、东南亚诸国及阿拉伯各国。福州同时还是沟通中国与海外文化交流的重要通道，印度般坦罗、日本圆珍等高僧曾到此学习交流佛学。福州在唐五代时期达到全盛，并与广州、扬州、明州并列为唐代的四大贸易港口。

◎ 闽王祠位于福州市鼓楼区庆城路，图为后殿考古现场。（福州市文物局供图）

Minwang Temple is on Qingcheng Road, Gulou District, Fuzhou City. The photo is of the archaeological site of the back hall. (Courtesy of Fuzhou Municipal Cultural Relics Bureau)

◎ "恩赐琅琊郡王德政碑"为唐天祐三年
（906）敕立，高5米，宽1.87米。碑
文记载了王审知家世及其治闽政绩，其
中多处记载了唐末五代福州与东南亚、
阿拉伯等地进行海外贸易的相关内容，
佐证了福州是海上丝绸之路的一个重要
节点。（福州市文物局供图）

The stele of Langya Lord was erected
in 906, standing at five metres tall and
1.87 metres wide. The inscriptions detail
Wang Shenzhi's genealogical history and
his political achievements while governing
Fujian. Many sections describe the trade
between Fuzhou, Southeast Asia and
Arab countries in the late Tang Dynasty
and during the Five Dynasties, proof that
Fuzhou was an important point along the
Maritime Silk Road. (Courtesy of Fuzhou
Municipal Cultural Relics Bureau)

In the late Tang Dynasty and the Five Dynasties, Wang Shenzhi encouraged foreign merchants to participate in maritime trade so that they continuously paid yearly tributes to the emperor. During the same time, he set up official offices to regulate cargo and levy taxes, and his brother Wang Chao established a taxation office, both of which helped to regulate maritime trade. During the 9th and 10th centuries, not only did Fuzhou pay tribute to the emperor in the form of exquisite textiles, but also traded silk, tea, paper and porcelain to the Korean Peninsula, Japan, Southeast Asian countries, and Arab countries. Fuzhou also became a centre for cultural exchanges, and people of great renown such as Japan's Enchin visited to learn about and exchange Buddhist teachings. It is during the Tang Dynasty and Five Dynasties that Fuzhou entered a golden age, and was named one of the four major trading ports alongside Guangzhou, Yangzhou, and Mingzhou.

■ 东方第一大港风采

后晋开运元年（944），"晋江王"留从效为保障泉州的对外贸易，继承王审知的策略，设立主管保护航线安全的海路都指挥使和主管市舶贸易的榷利院，鼓励公平买卖，拓展商业活动，对泉州港的发展有特殊的贡献。泉州也渐渐成为蕃客往来之地。唐朝廷为此专门在泉州设参军事四人，以管理海外来往的使节和商人。但此时的海上贸易以私人贸易为主。与此同时，大食帝国自阿拔斯王朝迁都巴格达后，大力发展海上贸易，加强与印度洋、东亚地区国家的海上商业往来。地处台湾海峡西岸的泉州，在唐中后期迅速发展成为中国南方的重要港口。

■ The Largest Port in the East

In the year 944 of the Later Jin Dynasty, the "Lord of Jinjiang" maintained Wang Shenzhi's philosophy to bolster Quanzhou's foreign trade. He established a customs office and coast patrol to maintain and protect trade routes, creating an environment that promoted open and fair trade, a legacy that contributed greatly to the development of Quanzhou Port, leading to its status as a cultural hub and trade destination. For this reason, the Tang court designated four military personnel in Quanzhou to manage the envoys and merchants, responsible for the majority of maritime trade. In the preceding centuries, the Abbasid Caliphate had relocated to Baghdad, and they too had invested significantly into maritime trade. Both they and China were able to make great use of the maritime trade routes, strengthening trade routes for countries in East Asia and across the Indian Ocean. Quanzhou, located on the west bank of Taiwan Strait, was poised perfectly to develop into one of the most important ports in China during the mid-late Tang Dynasty.

◎ 万寿塔位于石狮市永宁镇塔石村宝盖山山顶上，是泉州湾外海航标，主要解决商船通过台湾海峡主航道进出泉州港的指航需求。又名姑嫂塔，建于南宋绍兴年间（1131—1162），坐东向西，塔身用巨大的花岗岩块石构筑，空心，八角五层，通高 22.68 米。万寿塔抵御台风、暴风和地震，历经八百多年依然挺立，充分显示出宋代泉州建筑工匠的高超技艺。（泉州市文物局供图）

Located on the summit of Baogai Mountain in Tashi Village, Yongning Town of Shishi City, Wanshou Tower is a navigation landmark on the coast of Quanzhou Bay. Its primary purpose is to guide merchant ships travelling to and from Quanzhou Port through the Taiwan Strait. Also known as Gusao Tower, it was built during the Southern Song Dynasty, sometime in the years 1131—1162. Wanshou Tower is hollow, octagonal, and has five stories, standing 22.68m tall. Having stood through typhoons, storms and earthquakes for over 800 years, it is a fantastic example of the engineering prowess of the Song Dynasty. (Courtesy of Quanzhou Municipal Cultural Relics Bureau)

宋元时期，随着泉州港的迅速兴起，福建的对外交往开创了一个繁荣的时期。泉州以丝绸和陶瓷商品为大宗的海上贸易经历了从唐（7世纪初）到明初（15世纪末）前后长达九个世纪的辉煌历史。特别是北宋元祐二年（1087）设市舶司于泉州后，福州港的作用逐渐降低。泉州自北宋就是一个人口大州，而农耕面积却很小。在粮食危机与就业危机的压力下，泉州经济逐渐摆脱传统模式，走上弃农从商之路。前代发展起来的泉州港，与海外各国保持密切的通商贸易关系，同时面对新王朝建立后出现的更为广阔的国内市场，这一切都为泉州港在宋代的迅速发展创造了极好的环境。

With the rapid rise of Quanzhou Port during the Song and Yuan dynasties, Fujian entered a period of prosperity. The key trades of silk and ceramic goods lasted a glorious nine centuries, from the early 7th century to the late 15th century. In particular, during the year 1087, Quanzhou was designated as the major transport hub in the area, and Maritime Trade Office was established. Additionally, Quanzhou took over many duties of the nearby Fuzhou Port, which was wound down. Quanzhou had always been a populous city, despite limited farming land. Under the pressure of food shortage, Quanzhou's economy turned away from traditional agriculture and embraced trade as a more suitable alternative. Many generations of Quanzhou's population developed and maintained both foreign and domestic trade routes, creating an excellent environment for the growth of Quanzhou.

◎ 美山码头。（泉州市文物局供图）
Meishan Wharf. (Courtesy of Quanzhou Municipal Cultural Relics Bureau)

◎ 文兴码头。（泉州市文物局供图）
Wenxing Wharf. (Courtesy of Quanzhou Municipal Cultural Relics Bureau)

江口码头包含美山码头、文兴码头，均始建于宋代，位于泉州市丰泽区法石社区美山村和文兴村，处在江海交汇处的咽喉地带，是宋元时期泉州城区与港区水陆转运的枢纽，沿江的集群商业码头。20 世纪 50、80 年代，在此发现 12—15 世纪的造船遗址、船骸、石碇等以及数座伊斯兰教石墓。其中法石港宋船（未发掘）是继泉州湾后渚港海船出土之后的又一宋代海船重大发现。

Jiangkou Harbour is home to Meishan Wharf and Wenxing Wharf, both of which were built during the Song Dynasty, and are located in Meishan Village and Wenxing Village of Quanzhou respectively. Both villages are located at the mouth of the river, and together, formed the focal point of Quanzhou's trade district, owing to their commercial docks. In the 1950s and 1980s, shipbuilding sites, shipwrecks, stone inlays and several Islamic tombs from the 12th—15th centuries were discovered. Among them, a ship from the Song Dynasty that has yet to be excavated, was another critical discovery, providing information about the Song Dynasty, in addition to that provided to us by a ship found in Houzhu Port, Quanzhou.

◎ 伊斯兰教圣墓位于泉州丰泽区，占地面积约300平方米、安息着唐武德年间（618—626）来泉州传教的伊斯兰教先知穆罕默德的二位门徒"三贤""四贤"。泉州是伊斯兰教最早传入中国的地区之一，这里至今仍然生活着数以万计的阿拉伯人后裔，保留着浓郁的伊斯兰文化传统和众多史迹。（泉州市文物局供图）

The Islamic Tombs are located in Fengze District, Quanzhou, covering an area of 300 square metres. It is the resting place of two Islamic preachers, disciples of the prophet Muhammad, who came to Quanzhou during the years 618—626 of the Tang Dynasty. Quanzhou was one of the first regions of China to be introduced to Islam. There are still tens of thousands of Arab descendants living here, and there is a strong Islamic culture and many historical sites. (Courtesy of Quanzhou Municipal Cultural Relics Bureau)

　　宋末元初，泉州港并未遭受战争破坏，局势稳定之后还得到元朝统治者的特别照顾。首先批准重建福建市舶司（驻地泉州），仍由蒲寿庚担任。元至元十八年（1281）政府又规定：凡在泉州进口已在泉州交纳进出口税的货物，运至国内他处只交行商税而已。此时泉州相当于中国海关"总关"，标志着泉州港海外贸易进入全盛时期。

　　元中期，虽朝野政局动荡，泉州港时起时落，但仍保持着领先地位和发展趋势。然而，海外贸易的繁荣也不可避免地带来社会各阶层之间的矛盾冲突，再加上元朝末期的社会动荡，元末至正十七年（1357）到至正二十六年（1366），泉州爆发了持续十年之久的"亦思巴奚战乱"。这场战乱使得盛极一时的泉州港元气大损，泉州港开始走向没落。

Fortunately, in the transition from the Song Dynasty to the Yuan Dynasty, Quanzhou Port was not damaged by war. Despite this, after the imperial court had stabilised, the rulers of the Yuan Dynasty paid special attention to Quanzhou Port. The Maritime Trade Office was re-established in Quanzhou, and Pu Shougeng was continued as Superintendent of the office. In the year 1281, the government further decreed that goods imported in Quanzhou need only pay commercial tax upon being moved throughout the country—no additional levies would be charged. As a result, Quanzhou became the premier place for imports and exports, and was a de facto "General Customs Office" for China, greatly bolstering its importance in the Chinese economy.

Throughout the Yuan Dynasty, the political environment was volatile, and the development of Quanzhou Port moved with its ebb and flow. Despite this, Quanzhou's upward growth trend continued, maintaining its status. The prosperity was not to last, however. As trade brought ever growing opulence, so too did it bring inter-class conflict. Coupled with the social and political turmoil towards the end of the Yuan Dynasty, the Ispah rebellion took place. Lasting 10 years, from 1357 to1366, the civil wars caused irrecoverable damage to Quanzhou Port, and the standing that Quanzhou Port once held began to decline.

◎ 位于泉州鲤城区的清净寺建于北宋大中祥符二年（1009），是中国现存最古老的清真寺之一。现存建筑有门楼、奉天坛等，基本保持了宋元两代的建筑风格。南墙尖拱门上方有一列《古兰经》经文石刻，北墙尖拱门上额镶嵌清净寺始建及修建情况的古阿拉伯文石刻，壁龛内均浮雕《古兰经》铭文。（张清杰 摄）

Built in 1009, Qingjing Mosque in Quanzhou is one of China's oldest extant mosques. The gate, sacrificial altar and other parts of the building still remain, mostly of the architecture style of the Song and Yuan dynasties. Above each pointed arch on the south wall is a stone carving of excerpts of the Quran, and above the pointed arch on the north wall are stone carvings in Arabic, detailing the construction process of Qingjing Mosque, while readings from the Quran are carved in the niches. (Photo by Zhang Qingjie)

■ 郑和七下西洋

600多年前，受朝廷委派，郑和从明永乐三年（1405）至宣德八年（1433）统领舟师先后7次出使西洋，访问亚非30余国，舟师27,000多人，大小船只200多艘，宝船长44.4丈，宽18丈。郑和被公认为世界伟大的航海家，下西洋之时被定为中国航海日（7月11日）。

综观七下西洋全过程，郑和已经掌握的航海科技主要有：合理利用季风和洋流，运用"更"和"庹"分别计算航程和测量水深，使用罗盘定向、对景定位和地标导航，创造性地运用"过洋牵星"天文导航，观测和发现经度，绘制了《郑和航海图》。此举为世界航海史壮举，中国对外交流史的伟大发现，比哥伦布、达·伽马的地理大发现早半个世纪。航海规模之大，行程之远，足迹之广，历时之久，是当时任何国家无法比拟的。

◎ 圣寿宝塔位于福州市长乐区吴航镇南山，宋政和七年（1117）建成，八角七层楼阁式石塔，高27.4米，是郑和远眺太平港的瞭望塔，也是船队出入太平港的航标塔，是郑和下西洋事件的重要物证。它见证了中国与亚非国家友好交流的历史。（福州市文物局供图）

Shengshou Pagoda is located at Nanshan, Wuhang Town of Changle District, Fuzhou City. It was built in 1117 during the Song Dynasty. It is an octagonal seven-story pavilion stone tower, standing at 27.4 metres. The tower is important evidence of Zheng He's voyages to the West, having witnessed a history of friendly exchanges between China, Africa and other Asian countries. (Courtesy of Fuzhou Municipal Cultural Relics Bureau)

◎ 天妃灵应之记碑位于福州市长乐区吴航镇南
山，俗称"郑和碑"。明宣德六年（1431）
立，高 1.62 米，碑文 1177 字，详载郑和前
六次下西洋的经过及第七次下西洋的任务等
史实，是我国当今仅存的最原始详细记载郑
和航海史实的珍贵资料碑刻。（福州市文物
局供图）

Goddess Mazu's Answer Monument is located
in Nanshan, Wuhang Town of Changle District,
Fuzhou City, and is commonly known as "Zheng
He's Monument". Put up in 1431 during the
Ming Dynasty, it is 1.62m high and the inscription
is 1177 characters. It details important history,
such as Zheng He's seven voyages to the West.
It is the only original detailed record of Zheng
He's voyages, and is thus a precious artifact of
maritime history. (Courtesy of Fuzhou Municipal
Cultural Relics Bureau)

■ Zheng He's Seven Voyages to the West

More than 600 years ago, Zheng He was tasked by the imperial court with leading expeditions westward, from the years 1405—1433. He visited more than thirty countries across Asia and Africa, employing the help of over 27,000 sailors across 200 ships, with a flagship that boasted a length of 444 feet and width of 180 feet. He was recognised globally as a mariner and explorer, and the date of his departure to the west is now celebrated as China's National Maritime Day (July 11th).

In his ventures west, Zheng He mastered many navigation techniques, including taking advantage of ocean currents, charting effective routes and measuring water depth, the use of compasses and landmark navigation. The "Zheng He Navigation Chart" was created by observing stars to measure distance travelled. His heroic navigation is a significant feat among the history of world navigation, unmatched at the time, dating half a century before the great discoveries of Columbus and da Gama.

明代（1368—1644），福州是全国重要造船基地之一，造船工艺先进，装备精良。福州以太平港为主承接了郑和七下西洋船队在此驻泊与扬航。福建的丝绸、茶叶、瓷器等与海外交流愈加频繁，明成化年间（1465—1487）市舶司从泉州迁到福州，由此福州港地位迅速提升。

During the Ming Dynasty (1368—1644), Fuzhou was one of the most important shipbuilding bases in the country, with start of the art technology and equipment. Zheng He used Taiping Port as his home base from which he took his seven voyages. Fujian's silk, tea, and porcelain trade became largely based out of Fuzhou, and the Maritime Trade Office was moved from Quanzhou to Fuzhou during 1465 and 1487, which further led to the development of Fuzhou Port.

◎ 罗星塔位于福州市马尾区，早在明初就标绘在航海图中，是国际公认的海上重要航标之一。由于外国船来福州都在罗星塔下抛锚，外国水手把罗星塔称为"塔锚地"或"中国塔"。（包华 摄）
Standing as a landmark in Mawei District of Fuzhou at the mouth of the Min River, Luoxing Pagoda is an internationally recognized navigation mark. It was included in nautical charts over 600 years ago in the early Ming Dynasty. It was also called "Pagoda Anchorage" or "China Pagoda" by foreign sailors since their ships to Fuzhou anchored under the pagoda. (Photo by Bao Hua)

◎ 福州连江定海水下遗址出土了大批古代文物，包括从唐五代至明清时期的白瓷、青白瓷、黑釉瓷、青瓷、青花瓷器以及少量铜、铁、锡、木器等。其中定海白礁一号沉船遗址是一处以装载闽江下游窑址生产的黑釉瓷、青白瓷为主的宋元时期沉船遗址。定海湾沉船证明了这里是我国古代海上丝绸之路的重要组成部分，大量浙江、福建窑址生产的陶瓷器以及丝绸、茶叶等货物通过这片海域，沿着传统航线北上或南下销往东亚、东南亚，甚至远至西亚、欧洲、非洲等地，同时也将产自异域的香料等特产运进来，见证了我国古代海上交通贸易的繁荣与兴盛。（羊泽林 摄）

A large number of ancient relics were unearthed at the Dinghai Underwater Historic Site in Lianjiang, Fuzhou, including white porcelain, blue and white porcelain, black-glazed porcelain, celadon, blue porcelain, and some copper, iron, tin and wooden artifacts from the Tang Dynasty through to the Qing Dynasty. Here lies the shipwreck site of Dinghai Baijiao Number 1, a shipwreck from around the Song and Yuan dynasties, carrying a large amount of black-glazed and blue and white porcelain, produced at the kiln sites at the lower reaches of Min River. The shipwreck in Dinghai proves the importance of this location to the Maritime Silk Road. A large amount of ceramics, silk, tea and other goods produced at kiln sites in Zhejiang and Fujian would have passed through this area, before moving north or south along trade routes to other countries in Asia, as well as Europe and Africa. It was also the site of imports of products such as foreign spices, and remains a location of great contribution to China's ancient maritime trade. (Photo by Yang Zelin)

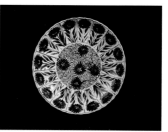

◎ 海坛海峡为古代海上丝绸之路交通要道，共确认 11 处水下文化遗存，年代序列完整，遗址类型多样，证实海坛海峡最迟在五代时期已经成为海上丝绸之路的重要航段，并且不间断地延续于之后的整个历史时期。海坛海峡水下文化遗存出水遗物丰富，生产窑口众多，反映不同历史时期中国陶瓷海外贸易状况，从中可以窥测中国古代贸易陶瓷外销的基本状况和大致脉络。（羊泽林 摄）

The Haitan Strait was an important part of the Maritime Silk Road. A total of 11 underwater relic sites have been confirmed. The ages and types of sites are wide ranging, proving the importance of the Strait from the Five Dynasties and Ten Kingdoms Period onwards. Haitan Strait's underwater relic sites contain a vast variety of artifacts, from various kiln sites, and are treasure troves that provide information about Chinese ceramics trade across history, allowing us to draw some general conclusions about the Chinese export trade of ceramics in the past. (Photo by Yang Zelin)

■ 漳州月港崛起

对于中国的航海史而言，漳州月港的历史并不算长，从 15 世纪中叶出人意料地崛起，到 17 世纪前半叶急剧衰落，前后不过一百余年。但是，在地理大发现的年代，月港的存在，对世界贸易的格局有着一定影响。

在明代实行海禁、仅允许部分对外开放沿海港口时期（16 世纪后半叶），漳州月港是合法的民间对外贸易港之一，拥有 7 条往西洋、3 条往东洋的直接航线，与东南亚、中南半岛以及朝鲜、琉球、日本等 47 个国家和地区有直接贸易往来，是我国东南沿海对外交通贸易中心，也是当时从中国经马尼拉（吕宋）至美洲的"海上丝绸之路"的主要起航港。

◎ 响馆码头是漳州月港现尚存的七
处码头之一，位于海澄月溪与九
龙江交汇处东侧，为当年外船申
报进出港临时停泊点。条石台阶
结构，伸入月溪口。（郑云 摄）
Xiangguan Wharf is one of the seven
surviving wharves in Zhangzhou
Yuegang Port. It is located on the
east side of the intersection of Yue
River and Jiulong River at Haicheng
Town. It was a temporary berthing
point for foreign ships, recording
traffic that entered and left the port.
The stone step structure extends
into Yue River. (Photo by Zheng Yun)

■ The Rise of Zhangzhou Yuegang Port

As far as the history of Chinese maritime navigation is concerned, the history of Yuegang Port is not long. From its unexpected rise in the middle of the 15th century to its sharp decline in the early 17th century, Yuegang Port only held significance for just over a hundred years. However, that is not to say it was not significant—in a time of great geographic discovery, the existence of Yuegang Port was certainly impactful.

During the Ming Dynasty, the government imposed strict maritime trade laws as part of its isolationist policy. One of the few legal private foreign trade ports, Yuegang Port had seven trade routes running west and three running east, connecting to the Indochina Peninsula, North Korea, the Ryukyu Islands, Japan and other countries and regions, totaling forty-seven, making it China's premiere foreign trading port on the Maritime Silk Road.

◎ 帆巷古街位于海澄镇豆巷村，是七大商市中旧桥头港市的一段，明末清初时期所建，迄今已有 400 多年历史。古街东边有月溪大船直通外海，西边有内河九十九湾，小船四通八达。古月港中的七个商市全被水网环绕，因此月港也被称作"海国"。（郑云 摄）

Fanxiang ancient street is located in Douxiang Village, Haicheng Town. Geographically located in the midst of seven major commercial towns, it was built during the late Ming and early Qing dynasties, boasting a history of over four centuries. On the east, there is Yue River, leading directly to the open sea, and on the west are 99 bends of the river, where small boats are plentiful. The seven major commercial towns around Yuegang Port are all surrounded by bodies of water, earning Yuegang the nickname "Country of the Sea". (Photo by Zheng Yun)

闽浙木拱廊桥（福建部分）
Wooden Arch Lounge Bridges
in Fujian and Zhejiang Provinces (Fujian Section)

◎ 屏南县万安桥下的游泳（郑家裕摄）
Swimming under Wan'an Bridge in Pingnan County (Photo by Yan Jiawei)

遗产价值

　　中国现存木拱廊桥 100 多座，主要分布于闽东北、浙南山区，是中国古代最具创造性和技术性的桥梁模式。福建最具代表性的木拱廊桥，有 12 座被列入《中国世界文化遗产预备名单》，包括宁德市寿宁县的鸾峰桥、大宝桥、杨梅州桥，宁德市周宁县的三仙桥，宁德市屏南县的广利桥、广福桥、千乘桥、龙津桥、万安桥，南平市政和县的赤溪桥、后山桥、洋后桥。

Universal Value

There are approximately 100 wooden arch lounge bridges in China, found primarily in northeastern Fujian and southern Zhejiang, each a testament to the engineering prowess of the Ming and Qing dynasties. Twelve are now part of various sites on China's UNESCO world heritage tentative list, an important first step in becoming recognised as a world heritage property, namely Luanfeng Bridge, Dabao Bridge, Yangmeizhou Bridge, Sanxian Bridge, Guangli Bridge, Guangfu Bridge, Qiancheng Bridge, Longjin Bridge and Wan'an Bridge located in Ningde, as well as Chixi Bridge, Houshan Bridge and Yanghou Bridge located in Nanping.

◎ 似彩虹跨涧的杨梅州桥。（许少华 摄）
Yangmeizhou Bridge, looking like a rainbow over the creek. (Photo by Xu Shaohua)

◎ 寿宁鸾峰桥是世界单跨最大的木拱廊桥。（许少华 摄）

Luanfeng Bridge in Shouning County has the longest single span of any bridge of its kind. (Photo by Xu Shaohua)

　　古代能工巧匠根据经验，总结出这种由短小构件通过榫卯搭接而成的拱架结构体系，在山地沟壑和水流湍急的溪涧飞架廊桥，解决了古代山区交通跨壑涉水的问题。木拱廊桥承载地域特色与桥梁结构技术于一身，将民俗文化、宗教信仰、经济社会沟通与其自身的交通功能融为一体，是闽东北浙南山区古代工匠和山居人民创造精神的代表作。

The use of mortise and tenon joints to connect wooden planks led to steady, stable and beautiful bridges. These bridges help people traverse gushing rivers, deep ravines, and mountainous terrain, connecting communities. Each bridge became not just a means of transport, but a reflection of local culture, a place to exchange information and beliefs, and a testament to the creativity, skill, and craftsmanship of the engineers of past in Fujian and Zhejiang provinces.

闽浙木拱廊桥是山地人居文化的杰出范例。它在取材、选址、施工等方面就地取材、因地制宜的特征，见证了古代山民长期与自然协调、斗争的互动过程；它是闽浙山区延续至今的风水文化的符号和象征，是村落中具有社会公共性的空间场所，是古代山村社会结构、经济组织、自我管理等乡土文化的映射。闽浙木拱廊桥的存在和保护虽然承受着现代社会发展的巨大压力，但仍具有不可忽视的价值和象征意义。

These bridges are also a symbol of the remarkable adaptability of the settlers of Fujian and Zhejiang, having undergone the critical process of site selection, material choice and sourcing as settlers tried to make the most of what was available to them. Each bridge has borne witness to the long-standing struggle of man vs nature, and now stand as proud monuments to the community. Wooden arch lounge bridges are used as a public place for local villagers, while a reflection of the local economic activity and a self-regulatory system. To this day, the wooden arch lounge bridges still have an important role to play in the communities of Fujian and Zhejiang, despite rapid advances in society and technology.

◎ 三仙桥，位于宁德市周宁县纯池镇禾溪村。明朝 1467 年始建，1917 年加宽重建。（李洪元 摄）
Sanxian Bridge, located in Hexi Village, Chunchi Town of Zhouning County, was built in 1467 and rebuilt in 1917. (Photo by Li Hongyuan)

◎ 政和县后山廊桥上当地村民供奉的观音。（王祥春 摄）
Worship of Bodhisattva Guanyin at Houshan Bridge in Zhenghe County. (Photo by Wang Xiangchun)

　　闽浙木拱廊桥作为聚落的"精神空间"，承载着山村乡民趋福避祸、祈求平安的信念，与山地人居延续至今的民间信仰直接关联。

　　闽浙木拱廊桥与北宋张择端《清明上河图》中所绘汴水虹桥在木拱结构体系上的相似性，是两者同属中国木拱桥体系的有力证明，从一个侧面反映出中国北宋时期木拱桥建造技术的先进和精湛，同时木拱廊桥在闽浙山区的大量遗存也为中国木拱桥建造技术的延续和演进提供了特殊的见证。

Wooden arch lounge bridges also serve as spiritual places in these communities, a place where villagers pray for safety, peace, and prosperity, and have close relationship with the local beliefs.

A comparison between the wooden arch lounge bridges of Fujian and Zhejiang and the one depicted in the famous painting "Along the River During the Qingming Festival" offers evidence that both subscribe to the same style of wooden arch bridge. While the painted bridge displays the aesthetic expression of the Song Dynasty, the bridges in Fujian and Zhejiang are a testament to the continually evolving engineering technology of the Chinese civilization.

木拱廊桥探幽

　　木拱廊桥文物本体分桥台、桥体、廊屋，最具标志性的是桥体结构，此外桥相关文物和历史环境要素包括桥山、桥田、桥林、桥约、桥碑、题记、桥匾、桥联等。其独特的结构特征主要表现在下部拱结构桥体上，它是由短小木构件榫卯搭接形成两种结构体系，并通过上下交叠编织组成大净跨、无拱柱结构，主要包括主拱圈和拱上结构。主拱圈是由单个短小杆件相贯形成的三节苗、五节苗两套拱肋系统相互穿插、相互承托，并通过横向牛头、剪刀撑联结成为近似板肋拱的特殊拱结构，它是桥体的主承重构件。拱上结构是辅助体系，由桥面系统、立柱以及剪刀撑、青蛙腿组成，分别放置于主拱圈的上面和两边。

◎ 龙津桥，位于屏南县后垅村。始建于清初，1847 年重建，桥长 33.5 米、宽 4.5 米，单孔跨度 23 米，桥东有碑记和夫人庙。（程水华 摄）
Longjin Bridge, rebuilt in 1847, lies in Houlong Village of Pingnan County. It is 33.5m long and 4.5m wide, and has a single span that stretches 23m long. On the east bridgehead there is a tablet inscription and a temple. (Photo by Cheng Shuihua)

The Charming Wooden Arch Lounge Bridges

Each wooden arch lounge bridge is composed of the abutment, iconic deck, and covered passageway. Other factors that contribute to the bridges' beauty include the surrounding environment and detailed inscriptions and carvings on the bridge. The uniqueness in structure of these bridges is found in the lower body, where clever use of mortise and tenon joints to form arch structures. The body is made up of three and five section arches, stabilised using cross beams, and bears the brunt of the load the bridge is put under. In addition to this, cross braces and wooden posts, called "frog-leg posts" in Chinese, support the primary structure, keeping it stable despite large spans.

◎ 龙津桥桥东的碑记。（程水华 摄）
The stone tablet inscription at the east bridgehead of Longjin Bridge. (Photo by Cheng Shuihua)

中国木拱桥传统营造技艺，2009 年被联合国教科文组织列入《急需保护的非物质文化遗产保护名录》。联合国教科文组织（UNESCO）在其官网的"中国木拱桥传统营造技艺"专页中评价道："木拱桥发现于中国东南沿海的福建省和浙江省。营造这些桥梁的传统设计与实践，融合了木材的应用、传统建筑工具、技艺、核心编梁技术和榫卯接合，以及一个有经验的工匠对不同环境和必要结构力学的了解。这种木工技艺需要通过绳墨的指导和其他工匠的配合执行才能完成。这种技艺通过口头、个人示范的方式来传承，或者通过师傅教授学徒、师傅教授家族内通过严格程序达成一致的宗亲等方式从一代传到下一代。这些家族在建造桥梁、维护桥梁和保护桥梁的过程里扮演着不可替代的角色。作为这项传统技艺的载体，木拱桥既是交通、交流工具，也是人们的聚会场所。它们是当地居民进行信息交流、娱乐、神俗信仰、深化人际关系、深化文化认同的重要聚会场所。这种由中国传统木拱桥创造的文化空间，提供了鼓励人与人之间交流、理解与尊重的环境。这种传统的衰落缘于最近几年的快速城市化、木材的减少和现有建筑空间的不足，这些原因结合起来，威胁到了这项技艺的传承与生存。"

In 2009, "Traditional design and practices for building Chinese wooden arch bridges" was inscribed into the List of Intangible Cultural Heritage in Need of Urgent Safeguarding by UNESCO. On its official website, UNESCO states "Wooden arch bridges are found in Fujian Province and Zhejiang Province, along China's southeast coast. The traditional design and practices for building these bridges combine the use of wood, traditional architectural tools, craftsmanship, the core technologies of 'beam-weaving' and mortise and tenon joints, and an experienced woodworker's understanding of different environments and the necessary structural mechanics. The carpentry is directed by a woodworking master and implemented by other woodworkers. The craftsmanship is passed on orally and through personal demonstration, or from one generation to another by masters teaching apprentices or relatives within a clan in accordance with strict procedures. These clans play an irreplaceable role in building, maintaining, and protecting the bridges. As carriers of traditional craftsmanship, the arch bridges function as both communication tools and venues. They are important gathering places for locals to exchange information, entertain, worship, and deepen relationships and cultural identity. The cultural space created by traditional Chinese arch bridges has provided an environment for encouraging communication, understanding and respect among human beings. The tradition has declined however in recent years due to rapid urbanization, scarcity of timber and lack of available construction space, all of which combine to threaten its transmission and survival."

目前已经严格确认的造桥家族有寿宁县徐氏和郑氏造桥世家、屏南县黄氏造桥世家、周宁县张氏造桥世家。

Prominent families that have been officially identified as masters of the craft include the Xu and Zheng families in Shouning County, the Huang family in Pingnan County, and the Zhang family in Zhouning County.

◎ 后陇桥所在的宁德市周宁县秀坑村，是远近闻名的"廊桥师傅村"，出了多位修建廊桥的名师傅。该桥为张氏造桥世家所建造。（张永艳 摄）

Xiukeng Village of Zhouning County is famous for its masters of the craft. Houlong Bridge in the picture was constructed by the Zhang family. (Photo by Zhang Yongyan)

◎ 长桥飞架，壮观万安桥。（傅熹 摄）
The magnificent Wan'an Bridge. (Photo by Fu Xi)

■ 万安桥

　　万安桥位于宁德市屏南县长桥镇长桥村，始建于北宋元祐五年（1090），现存桥体于 1932 年重建。桥五墩六孔，桥长 98.2 米，宽 4.7 米，净跨 10.8—14.85 米，是中国现存所载始建年代最早、桥身最长的木拱廊桥。有桥屋 38 开间，用柱 156 根，两侧设有长条木椅，供村民们休憩谈笑。正中有嵌入桥墩的石碑，记载了建桥的人家、缘由、费用、时间等信息；桥屋内檐下有 13 副楹联，盛赞了长桥飞架的景观，为后人留下了珍贵的人文资料。万安桥净跨大，桥孔多，技术难度大，对研究古桥梁建筑具有重大价值。

■ Wan'an Bridge

Located in Changqiao Village of Pingnan County, Wan'an Bridge was originally constructed in 1090 during the Northern Song Dynasty, the present bridge was rebuilt in 1932. Consisting of five piers, the bridge is 98.2m long, 4.7m wide and has spans ranging from 10.8 to 14.85 metres. It is China's oldest and longest wooden arch lounge bridge. The deck has 38 windows on either side and uses 156 pillars to support the roof. Along the sides run long wooden benches, where locals can relax, converse, and socialise. At the centre pier of the bridge is a stele that commemorates the builders, contributions, construction date and resources, and the bridge's reason to be. Under the eaves of the covered passageway are thirteen couplets that describe the beauty of the surrounds and pass on cultural heritage to future generations. Wan'an Bridge has large spans, uses many piers, and is a prime example of overcoming many technical difficulties, giving us valuable insight into the architecture of generations past.

◎ 拾阶而上，穿斗式梁架飞檐走梭，气势雄伟。（颜家蔚 摄）

The beams, eaves and roofs are quite imposing. (Photo by Yan Jiawei)

◎ 嵌入桥墩的石碑碑记见证着万安桥的历史。（戴志坚 摄）

The inscription on the central pier is a record of the construction information of the bridge. (Photo by Dai Zhijian)

■ 千乘桥

千乘桥位于宁德市屏南县棠口乡棠口村，建于清嘉庆二十五年（1820）。桥一墩二孔，桥长62.7米，宽4.9米，净跨26.48—28.74米。周边的祥峰寺、文昌阁、夫人宫、三圣夫人宫、林公庙、"节孝"石牌坊、齐天大圣庙、土地庙、八角亭等，共同构成了棠口村极富历史感的公共空间。

■ Qiansheng Bridge

Built in 1820 during the Qing Dynasty, Qiansheng Bridge is in Tangkou Village, Pingnan County. With a single pier, the bridge is 62.7m long, 4.9m wide and boasts spans of 26.48m and 28.74m. Along with the bridge, the surrounding area also contains Xiangfeng Temple, Wenchang Pavilion, Furen Temple, Sansheng Furen Temple, Lingong Temple, Jiexiao Stone Arch, Qitian Temple, Tudi Temple, Bajiao Pavilion etc., making Tangkou Village a place of significant historical and cultural value.

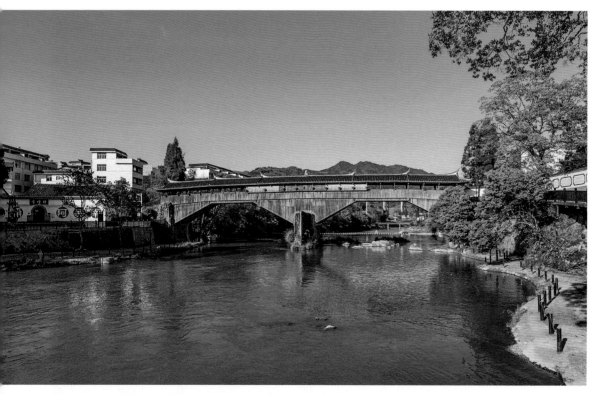

◎ 至今仍为交通要道的千乘桥。（颜家蔚 摄）
Qiansheng Bridge stills serves as a major road. (Photo by Yan Jiawei)

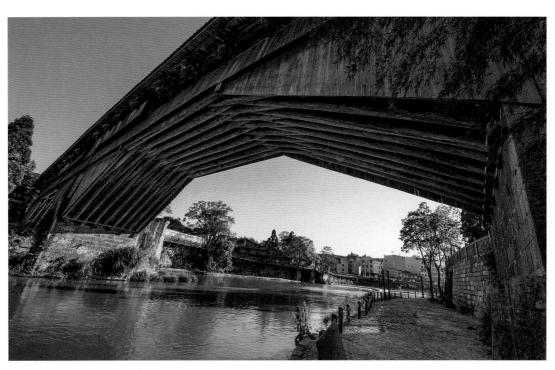

◎ 气势恢宏的桥拱。（颜家蔚 摄）

The arch of Qiansheng Bridge. (Photo by Yan Jiawei)

◎ 桥旁的棠口八角亭。（程水华 摄）

The Bajiao Pavilion by Qiansheng Bridge. (Photo by Cheng Shuihua)

■ 杨梅州桥

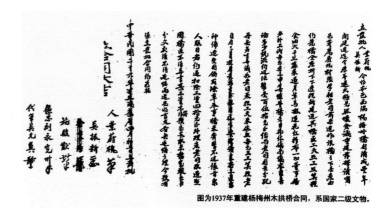

图为1937年重建杨梅州木拱桥合同，系国家二级文物。

杨梅州桥位于宁德市寿宁县坑底乡杨梅州村，建于清乾隆五十六年(1791)。桥单孔，桥长42.5米，宽4.64米，净跨33.75米。桥与周边环境融为一体，四季景观优美。清道光二十一年（1841年）和民国二十六年（1937年）两次造桥的桥约是国内木拱廊桥留有两份桥约见证的孤例。

◎ 1937年重建杨梅州桥的桥约，系国家二级文物。（龚迪发 征集）
Agreement for refurbishment in 1937 is a national relic. (Courtesy of Gong Difa)

■ Yangmeizhou Bridge

Found in Yangmeizhou Village, Shouning County, this bridge was built in 1791 during the Qing Dynasty. The bridge is 42.5m long, with a span of 33.75m, and is 4.64m wide. Complemented perfectly by its surroundings, it is beautiful all year round. Agreements for refurbishment in both 1841 and 1937 are the only two of their kind on record to date in China.

◎ 木拱桥梁架上书有建桥工匠的姓名。（许少华 摄）
The woodworkers' names were inscribed on the beams. (Photo by Xu Shaohua)

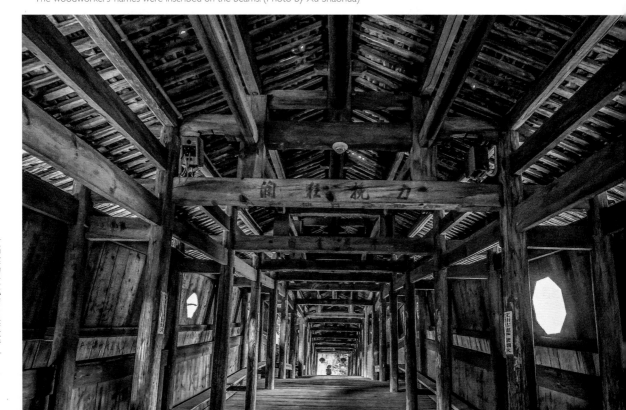

■ 鸾峰桥

　　鸾峰桥位于宁德市寿宁县下党乡下党村，重建于清嘉庆五年（1800）。桥单孔，桥长 47.6 米，宽 4.9 米，净跨 37.6 米。单跨距离为全国之最，桥址绝险，是寿宁现存最长最壮观的木拱廊桥。

■ Luanfeng Bridge

Rebuilt in 1800 during the Qing Dynasty, Luanfeng Bridge is located in Xiadang Village, Shouning County. At 47.6m long and 4.9m wide, this bridge boasts the longest single span distance in China, at 37.6m. Perched on a precarious site, Luanfeng Bridge is the most stunning bridge in the county.

◎ 春华秋实映古桥。（许少华 摄）
Picturesque Luanfeng Bridge. (Photo by Xu Shaohua)

■ 大宝桥

大宝桥位于宁德市寿宁县坑底乡小东村，建于清光绪四年（1878），桥长44.3米，宽4.6米，净跨33.1米。桥上彩绘、墨书丰富，是重要的人文资料。为了抵御洪水，在较宽阔的一侧桥墩巧妙设计了倒"V"字形的分流石砌桥墩，并在该桥头设计了"U"字形的泄洪口。

■ Dabao Bridge

Located in Xiaodong Village, Shouning County, Dabao Bridge was built in 1878 during the Qing Dynasty. Standing at 44.3m long, 4.6m wide with a span of 33.1m, Dabao Bridge contains a number of cultural artifacts, including colourful paintings and ink writings of old. Built to be flood-resistant, a cleverly designed inverted V-shaped structure was implemented on the wider side of the bridge, and a U-shaped spillway implemented under the bridgehead.

◎ 大宝桥的防洪设计最为巧妙。（许少华 摄）
Dabao Bridge was cleverly designed. (Photo by Xu Shaohua)

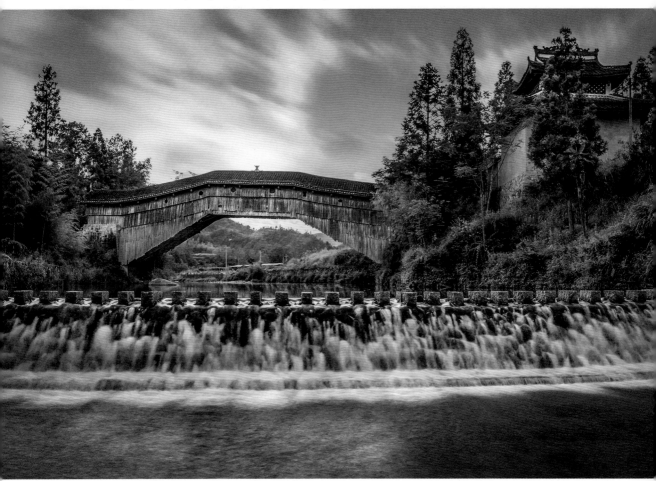

◎ 如诗如画广利桥。（许少华 摄）
Enchanting Guangli Bridge. (Photo by Xu Shaohua)

■ 广利桥和广福桥

　　广利桥和广福桥均位于宁德市屏南县岭下乡岭下村，相距仅 800 余米，是少有的姐妹桥。广利桥重建于清乾隆三十九年（1774），桥长 28.33 米，桥宽 4.33 米，净跨 19.19 米。桥东有一通碑记，记载了捐建人的姓名和金额。

■ Guangli Bridge and Guangfu Bridge

Located in Lingxia Village of Pingnan County, these rare sister bridges are only 800m apart. Guangli Bridge was rebuilt in 1774 during the Qing Dynasty. It is 28.33m long, 4.33m wide and has a span of 19.19m. To the east of the bridge is a monument that records the contributions made by dozens of people towards the construction of the bridge.

广福桥重建于清嘉庆十二年（1807），桥长 29.67 米，宽 4.75 米，净跨 24.17 米。两岸古树名木参天，还有千年古寺景福寺，显得清幽秀丽。

Guangfu Bridge was reconstructed a short while later, in 1807. It is 29.67m long, 4.75m wide and has a span of 24.17m. Towering trees surround the bridge on either side, and with the thousand-year-old Jingfu Temple in the background—it is a scene of serenity and elegance.

◎ 清幽秀丽广福桥。（许少华 摄）
The bridge is serene and beautiful. (Photo by Xu Shaohua)

◎ 赤溪桥侧影。（徐庭盛 摄）
Side view of Chixi Bridge. (Photo by Xu Tingsheng)

■ 赤溪桥

　　赤溪桥位于南平市政和县澄源乡赤溪村，全长 33.5 米，面宽 4.8 米，净跨 24 米。唐朝著名书法家颜真卿的后裔择居此处，繁衍四十余代。颜氏子孙于清乾隆五十五年（1790）建该桥，清嘉庆二十三年（1818）重修，并在梁架上留有墨书加以记载。

■ Chixi Bridge

Chixi Bridge is located in Chixi Village of Zhenghe County in Nanping City. It is 33.5m long, 4.8m wide and has a span of 24m. The descendants of the famous calligrapher Yan Zhenqing of the Tang Dynasty have lived here for more than forty generations. They first built the bridge in 1790 during the Qing Dynasty, and rebuilt it in 1818, the records of which are detailed on the bridge frame in ink.

■ 后山桥

后山桥位于南平市政和县岭腰乡后山村，建于清嘉庆四年（1799），全长 41.6 米，面宽 4.9 米，净跨 32 米。古桥美观坚固，横梁、枋木上依稀可见古字古画，栏板上有方形、葫芦形、桃形等不同形状的花窗，桥两头燕尾橼角高高翘起。

■ Houshan Bridge

Located in Houshan Village, Zhenghe County, Houshan Bridge was built in 1799 during the Qing Dynasty. It is 41.6m long, 4.9m wide and has a span of 32m. Steady and strong, the bridge has a timeless beauty, accented by faint but visible inscriptions. With uniquely shaped windows and raised rafters on either side, Houshan Bridge exhibits an effortless gracefulness.

◎ 画中后山桥。（余明传 摄）
Houshan Bridge and the surroundings are truly picturesque. (Photo by Yu Mingchuan)

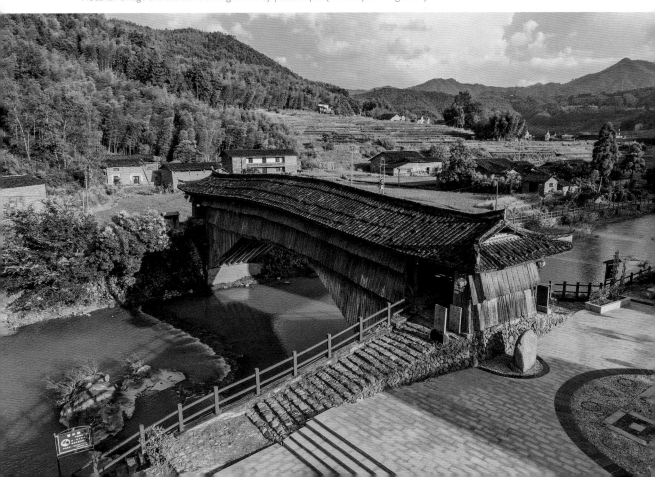

■ 洋后桥

　　洋后桥位于南平市政和县外屯乡外屯村，建于清道光三十年（1850），桥长 34 米，宽 5 米，净跨 27.7 米。桥顶檩上仍可见重建时留下的墨书，建桥工匠以许进何为主墨。桥南端与依山而建的寺庙相接。

■ Yanghou Bridge

Positioned near Waitun Village of Zhenghe County in Nanping City, this bridge was built in 1850 during the Qing Dynasty. It is 34m long, 5m wide and has a span of 27.7m. On the purlins are traces of ink writing from reconstruction efforts, and at the southern end of the bridge is a temple at the base of the mountain.

◎ 静静的洋后桥。（戴志坚 摄）
The calm and peaceful Yanghou Bridge. (Photo by Dai Zhijian)

闽南红砖建筑
The Red Brick Buildings of Southern Fujian

◎ 规模宏大的蔡氏古民居建筑群是闽南红砖建筑的典型代表。（张梓昌 摄）
The Cai family residence is a typical large-scale example of the red brick buildings of Southern Fujian. (Photo by Zhang Zichang)

遗产价值

　　分布在中国东南沿海的闽南红砖建筑，是伴随闽南文化的发展从中国传统民居演变而来的独特民居形态。闽南人重视以宗族传统为代表的中国传统文化的传承，反映出传统制度对闽南民居建筑的深远影响。海洋文化外向性特质又造就了这些聚落与众不同的浓烈色彩、大胆夸张的建筑造型和对建筑装饰的由衷热爱。闽南红砖聚落是闽南传统文化的突出见证。这一民居聚落形态对之后闽南地区以及周边区域的建筑风格产生了较深远的影响。

　　以南安蔡氏古民居和大嶝郑氏聚落为代表的闽南红砖建筑于 2012 年被列入《中国世界文化遗产预备名单》。闽南红砖聚落铭刻着他们古老家族的血脉渊源，见证了各个宗族历经迁徙，应对地域环境和社会变迁的不断挑战，最终形成一个既饱含深厚传统文化底蕴，又有强烈外向性，极具开拓精神的文化群体的历程。闽南红砖建筑真实展现了闽南福佬民系及其特有的民居聚落形态相伴相生的发展过程。

◎ 浓烈的红色是闽南建筑特色之一。（陈英杰 摄）
The strong red color is one of the distinctive characteristics of Southern Fujian buildings. (Photo by Chen Yingjie)

◎ 蔡氏古民居建筑群丰富
　　而精美的雕饰。（南安
　　市委宣传部 供图）

Diverse and exquisite
carvings in the Cai Family
Residence. (Courtesy of
the Publicity Department
of Nan'an Municipal
Committee of the CPC)

Universal Value

Dotted along the southeast coast of China, the red brick buildings of Southern Fujian are a unique style of residential architecture that has developed with the culture of Fujian. They are unique residential buildings derived from Chinese traditional residential buildings. The people of Southern Fujian place great importance on passing on clan tradition, a representation of Chinese traditional culture, showing the profound impact of traditional system on Southern Fujian residential architecture. The extroverted nature of marine culture here contributed to the distinctive strong colouring, bold, exaggerated architectural style and a sincere love of architectural ornaments. The red brick buildings of Southern Fujian are a true representation of Southern Fujian traditional culture, having a longlasting impact on the architectural style of the entire region and the surrounding area.

The Cai Family Residence in Nan'an City and the Zheng Family Residence in Dadeng Town were listed on China's UNESCO world heritage tentative list in 2012. They are perfect examples of Southern Fujian red brick buildings, engraving their clan's kinship. They have witnessed the journey of many families and clans to form a community, rich in traditional culture, extraversion and pioneering spirit. On the journey, the clans experienced challenges both natural and manmade. The red brick buildings of Southern Fujian are a true reflection of the history of the Hoklo ethnic group, and their journey to where they are today.

红砖古厝寻踪

■ 蔡氏古民居

　　蔡氏古民居位于南安市官桥镇，由蔡启昌及其子蔡资深（乳名"浅"）兴建。大约30,000平方米的长方形地块中，东西道长200多米，南北通宽100多米。东部和西部之间设有院墙和院门。为了防御和保障聚落整体安全性，设有围墙、炮楼、哨门等防御性设施，内部还有召集聚落成员和传递信息的钟鼓楼，有处理宗族各项事宜的宗祠，有当铺、公共食堂、公共柴火间和焙制花生的作坊等；在聚落南北设果园，东、南、西面置田地。

　　建筑群保护范围内现存的清代民居共20座，其中以现存蔡资深所建的16座建筑最具特色，包括世祐厝、世双厝、醉经堂、德棣厝、攸楫厝、启昌厝、德梯厝、彩楼厝、德典别馆、德典厝、蔡浅别馆、世用厝、蔡浅厝、当铺、孝友第、宗祠。

◎ 蔡氏古民居总建筑面积约 16,300 平方米。（张艺欣 摄）
The total floor area of the Cai Family Residence covers 16,300m². (Photo by Zhang Yixin)

Visiting the Ancient Red Brick Houses

■ Cai Family Residence

The Cai Family Residence is located in Guanqiao Town of Nan'an City, built by Cai Qichang and his son Cai Zishen, whose infant name is Qian. It sits on a piece of land that is over 200m long in the east-west direction, and over 100m long in the north-south direction, for a total area of approximately three hectares. The residence is divided into east and west parts by gates and walls. To defend from attack, there are defensive facilities in place on the outer perimeter, including walls, defensive towers and sentry gates. In the inner courtyards there are drum and bell towers to gather residents and exchange information. The residence also has many civilian facilities, including the ancestral hall to deal with matters of the clan, the pawnshop, the canteen and individual workstations such as peanut roasting workshops, storage buildings such as communal firewood storage. There are also orchards to both the north and south of the settlement, and fields to the east, west and south.

There are twenty extant buildings from the Qing Dynasty under protection within the building complex. Among them, the 16 built by Cai Zishen are particularly distinctive. They are Shiyou House, Shishuang House, Zuijing House, Dedi House, Youji House, Qichang House, Deti House, Cailou House, Dedian Villa, Dedian House, Caiqian Villa, Shiyong House, Caiqian House, Xaioyoudi House, the pawnshop, and the ancestral hall.

◎ 世祐厝建于 1889 年前后，建筑面积约 642 平方米，二进五开间带东西护厝。门廊正面和侧面嵌有整幅的砖雕，东护厝花厅檐下施精美雕塑。大厅两侧隔屏木刻"二十四孝"，雕刻精美，形态生动。（成冬冬 摄）

Shiyou House was built around 1889 and covers an area of about 642 square metres. It is five rooms wide, with two courtyards and two rows of guardhouses on both east and west sides. The front and lateral sides of the portico are decorated by whole brick sculptures. On the eaves of the parlor in the east guardhouse there are beautiful sculptures. The wood partitions on both sides of the main hall are exquisitely carved with "the Twenty-four Filial Exemplars". (Photo by Cheng Dongdong)

◎ 世双厝建于 1886 年前后，建筑面积约 642 平方米，二进五开间带东西护厝。主建筑为硬山顶，燕尾脊，穿斗式构架，红墙碧瓦。门廊正面与两侧各嵌砖雕灵禽瑞兽，刀法粗犷古朴。大厅两侧木隔扇上有精美的雕刻。下图为世双厝门廊侧面的砖雕。（成冬冬 摄）

Shishuang House was built approximately in 1886, covering an area of about 642 square metres. It is five rooms wide, with two courtyards and two rows of guardhouses on both east and west sides, the same as Shiyou House. The main building features a gabled roof, a swallowtail ridge and column and tie construction with red walls and green tiles. The front and sides of the portico are decorated by brick sculptures of various birds and animals. The wood partitions on both sides of the main hall are exquisitely carved. The following is a picture of brick sculptures on the side of the portico of Shishuang House. (Photo by Cheng Dongdong)

◎ 德棣厝建于 1893 年前后，建筑面积约 1,068 平方米，三进五开间带东西护厝。主建筑硬山顶，燕尾脊，穿斗式构架，红墙碧瓦。屋脊堆三彩花鸟，为建筑群中仅见。图中德棣厝东北角两层的读书楼，以小拱门与正屋相通。（张梓昌 摄）

Dedi House was built around 1893, covering an area of about 1,068 square metres. It is five rooms wide, with three courtyards and two rows of guardhouses on both east and west sides. The main building has a gabled roof, a swallowtail ridge and column and tie construction with red walls and green tiles. The ridge is decorated with tri-color birds and flower sculptures, which is the only one among the Cai family residence complex. The above picture shows the two-storey study in the northeast corner of the house, connected to the main hall via a small archway. (Photo by Zhang Zichang)

◎ 醉经堂位于建筑群最东端，约建于1911年，建筑面积约244平方米，面阔三间，进深三进，规模小而布局完整。大门匾书"醉经堂"，檐下彩绘人物故事。门廊上部彩绘人物，中部墨书诗文。室内装饰精美，门厅两侧彩绘山水花鸟和名人题词相间。左图为大门侧面所嵌砖雕人物故事。（成冬冬 摄）

Zuijing House is located at the easternmost end of the Cai family residence complex. It was built around 1911 and covers an area of about 244 square metres. It is three rooms wide with three courtyards. Although small, it is well decorated and complete. The plaque at the gate reads "Zuijingtang", and a figure story is painted along its eaves. Above the doorframe are more painted figures, while there are lines of Chinese poetry around the doorframe. The interior of the house is decorated elaborately, with multi-themed colored paintings on both sides. The left are pictures of brick sculptures on the sides of the portico. (Photo by Cheng Dongdong)

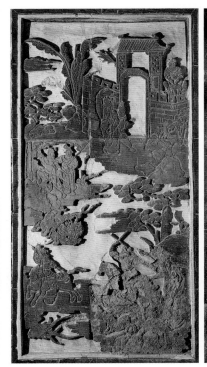

◎ 攸楫厝建于 1867 年前后，为建筑群中最早的建筑之一。建筑面积约 719 平方米，三进五开间带东西护厝。立面檐下彩绘人物与花鸟，门廊两侧彩绘人物故事与砖雕灵禽瑞兽相间。（张梓昌 摄）

Youji House was built around 1867 and joins Qichang House as one of the oldest in the complex. It covers an area of about 719 square metres and shares a similar layout plan to Qichang house, with five rooms wide, three courtyards and two rows of guardhouses on both east and west sides. The eaves are decorated with paintings of flora, birds and humans. The sides of the portico are painted with celebrity stories and decorated by brick sculptures of various birds and animals. (Photo by Zhang Zichang)

◎ 启昌厝约建于 1867 年前后，为建筑群中最早建筑之一。建筑面积约 719 平方米，三进五开间带东西护厝。堂前隔屏贴金木雕透视感极强，隔扇墨书治家格言，反映儒家立德、立功、立言的道德要求，为建筑群中仅见。屋宇内外多处饰有鱼尾狮，反映了南洋建筑装饰艺术的影响。图为启昌厝门廊上精美的彩绘和泥塑。（成冬冬 摄）

Qichang House was built around 1867 and is one of the oldest buildings in the complex. It is about 719 square metres, with five rooms wide, three courtyards and two rows of guardhouses on both east and west sides. The partitions in the front of the main hall are well decorated with gilded wood sculptures, and inked with the family values, which is the only one among the Cai Family Residence complex. There are statues of merlions scattered throughout the buildings, influenced by the Nanyang architectural style. The photo shows the exquisite coloured paintings and clay sculptures above the doorframe of Qichang House. (Photo by Cheng Dongdong)

◎ 德梯厝建于 1889 年前后，建筑面积约 627 平方米，二进五开间带东西护厝。墙面饰有砖刻八仙，形态逼真，别具一格。立面檐下施泥塑村居景物，门廊彩绘石雕人物、花鸟多重组合。（张梓昌 摄）

Deti House was built around 1889, covering an area of about 627 square metres. It is five rooms wide, with two courtyards and two rows of guardhouses on both east and west sides. The walls are decorated with carvings of the Eight Immortals, each vivid and unique. The clay sculptures of scenery are placed outside under the eaves of the facade. The portico's stone carvings are of various people, birds and flowers. (Photo by Zhang Zichang)

◎ 彩楼厝建于 1889 年前后，建筑面积约 682 平方米，三进五开间带西护厝。立面檐下施泥塑，彩绘相衬。门廊石雕人物、山水多重组合。厅堂隔屏木雕为贴金博古图案。二、三进间筑小亭相连，歇山屋顶作葱头形山花，反映受伊斯兰文化艺术的影响。（张梓昌 摄）

Cailou House was built around 1889, covering about 682 square metres. It is five rooms wide, with three courtyards and a guardhouse on the west. Clay sculptures are under the eaves here, complemented by colourful paintings. The stone sculptures through the portico depict people and beautiful scenery and the partitions in the living room are decorated with gilded wood sculptures of traditional patterns. The second and third courtyards are connected by a small pavilion. The pediment of hip and gable roof looks like an onion bulb, influenced by Islamic culture and aesthetics. (Photo by Zhang Zichang)

◎ 德典厝建于 1908 年前后，建筑面积约 863 平方米，三进五开间带西护厝。门廊石雕、木雕相衬，人物、花鸟共喧，正面与两侧各嵌辉绿岩雕，刀法纯熟，线条流畅。厅堂中陈列着整套当年遗留下来的香案、供桌和祭器。二、三进之间筑卷棚轩盖小亭相连，为群体中仅见。（张梓昌 摄）

Dedian House was built around 1908, covering about 863 square metres. It is five rooms wide, with three courtyards and a guardhouse on the west. The stone and wood sculptures throughout the portico depict people, flowers and birds. There are also diabase carvings with smooth lines, carved clearly and skillfully. The main hall displays incense tables and altars from past. The second and third courtyards are connected by a small roll-up shed pavilion, which is the only one among the Cai Family Residence complex. (Photo by Zhang Zichang)

◎ 世用厝建于 1907 年前后，建筑面积约 1,182 平方米。正屋三进，东为护厝，西为花厅，花厅北段筑小楼，集中体现了闽南古民居建筑的形制。门廊顶部饰有青石浮雕人物故事，檐下嵌山水花鸟画。（张梓昌 摄）

Shiyong House was built around 1907, covering about 1,182 square metres. There are three courtyards with a guardhouse on the east and a parlour on the west, north of which is a small residential building, prime examples of the ancient residential buildings of Southern Fujian. The portico roof is decorated with bluestone relief figures, and below the eaves are carved landscapes, embedded with flowers and birds. (Photo by Zhang Zichang)

◎ 蔡浅别馆建于 1904 年前后，为蔡资深归老故园之别馆，建筑面积约 680 平方米，二进五开间带西护厝。厅堂正面隔扇上书一"寿"字，高 1.1 米，宽 0.62 米，四角浮雕蝙蝠，雄浑古朴。（张梓昌 摄）

Caiqian Villa was built around 1904 as a villa for Cai Zishen returning from the Philippines. The building covers about 680 square metres. It is five rooms wide, with two courtyards and a guardhouse on the west. The frontal partition of the main hall gets a Chinese character "Shou (longevity)" on it, measuring 1.1m high and 0.62m wide. The four corners of the partition are embossed with bat reliefs, indicating good fortune. (Photo by Zhang Zichang)

◎ 蔡浅厝建于 1893 年前后，完成于 1903 年，为蔡资深归老所居，占地 1,250 平方米，建筑面积约 878 平方米。整座建筑轴线对称，等级分明，布局完整，雕饰精美，处处显现当时闽南民间建筑高超技艺及受南洋装饰文化的影响。图为蔡浅厝内外景。（成冬冬 摄）

Caiqian House was constructed around 1893 and completed in 1903. It was also a dwelling place for Cai Zishen after his retirement. It claims 1,250 square metres, and the building itself covers about 878 square metres. The complex is perfectly symmetrical, logically laid out. It boasts beautiful carvings, a display of the incredible skill of local architecture and interior design of the time, heavily influenced by Nanyang decorative styles. The pictures show the house from various angles. (Photo by Cheng Dongdong)

◎ 孝友第建于 1907 年前后，建筑面积约 1,216 平方米，三进五开间。建筑南北分别有护厝和花厅一列。这是蔡浅的三个儿子共居之所。孝友第是整个建筑群中建筑面积最大的一座。（张梓昌摄）

Xiaoyoudi House was built around 1907, covering approximately 1,216 square metres. It is five rooms wide with three courtyards. On both the north and south sides there are a guardhouse and a parlour. Xiaoyoudi House is where Cai Qian's three sons lived together and is the largest building of the Cai Family Residence complex. (Photo by Zhang Zichang)

■ 大嶝郑氏聚落

    大嶝郑氏聚落位于厦门翔安区大嶝岛田墘村，包括大嶝抗战时期金门县政府旧址群12栋建筑（1937年金门沦陷后，国民党金门县政府从金门迁到大嶝，1945年抗战胜利，金门县政府从大嶝迁回金门）和其他价值较高的民居及私塾5栋，共17栋建筑。其中最有代表性的为大嶝金门县政府旧址群（包括金门县政府总部、金门县政府文书房、金门县政府会议旧址、金门县政府保安队队址、国民党金门县党部书记处、金门县政府盐兵楼和国民党金门县党部）。

◎ 大嶝金门县政府旧址群总占地面积 2,111.6 平方米，总建筑面积 2,698.6 平方米。（郑水忠 摄）
The former site of Jinmen County Government Complex in Dadeng covers 2,111.6 square metres, and a total floor space of 2,698.6 square metres. (Photo by Zheng Shuizhong)

◎ 金门县政府总部位于田墘北里131号、132号和137号。131号和132号为金门县政府总部的办公场所，137号则是作为金门县政府会客厅。田墘北里131号建筑坐东朝西，面宽11.4米，进深21米，建筑面积约239.4平方米。131号建筑外墙墙裙为花岗岩条石砌成，墙身为红砖砌筑。门厅前落面阔3间，进深1间，明间为厅，两侧为厢房。屋顶为硬山顶，屋脊起翘呈燕尾式。（郑水忠 摄）

Jinmen County Government Headquarters are located at Nos. 131, 132, and 137 of Tianqian North Road. Buildings of Nos. 131 and 132 served as office space, whereas No. 137 was an important meeting place. The building of No. 131 itself faces west, measuring 11.4m wide and 21m deep, covering an area of about 239.4 square metres. The dado of Building 131 is made of granite, and the wall is of red brick. The front courtyard is three rooms wide and one room deep, with a central, bright room designated as the main hall and two wing rooms. The building is set up with gabled roof and swallowtail ridge. (Photo by Zheng Shuizhong)

■ Zheng Family Residence in Dadeng Town

The Zheng Family Residence is situated in Tianqian Village, Dadeng Island of Xiang'an District, Xiamen City. It includes 12 buildings that had belonged to the Jinmen County Government during the War of Resistance against Japanese Aggression; after the fall of Jinmen in 1937, the Kuomintang Jinmen County Government moved to Dadeng, before moving back after the war ended in 1945. The Zheng Family Residence also includes five other historically valuable buildings, which are private residences and schools, totaling seventeen invaluable historical buildings. Of them, the most representative is the former site of the Jinmen County Government Complex, which includes Jinmen County Government Headquarters, Jinmen County Government Secretariat Office, Former Site of Jinmen County Government Conference, Former Site of Jinmen County Government Security Force Headquarters, Office of Kuomintang's Jinmen County Party Secretariat, Jinmen County Government Defensive Fort, and Kuomintang's Jinmen County Party Office.

◎ 田墘北里 132 号建筑为闽南传统红砖建筑，坐东朝西，面宽 11.6 米，进深 19.6 米，建筑面积约 227.4 平方米。正厅设有木雕祖龛，祖龛高 3 米，宽 3.5 米，用材为樟木和檀香木，整座祖龛精雕细刻并施以漆金。屋顶为硬山顶，屋脊起翘呈燕尾式。（蔡健 摄）

Building of No. 132 is in the traditional red brick style of Southern Fujian. It faces west, measuring 11.6m wide and 19.6m deep, covering about 227.4 square metres. There is a wooden ancestral tablet in the main hall, standing at 3m tall and 3.5m wide. It is made of camphor wood and sandalwood, exquisitely carved and lacquered with gold. The building is of gabled roof and swallowtail ridge. (Photo by Cai Jian)

◎ 田墘北里137号为两层闽南传统红砖建筑，坐东朝西，面宽8.4米，进深5.7米，建筑面积约82.3平方米。一层外墙墙裙为花岗岩条石砌成，墙身为红砖砌筑。屋顶为硬山顶，屋脊呈马鞍式，屋面以红色板瓦铺就。137号建筑大门门额题"万桂联芳"四字。（郑水忠 摄）

Building of No. 137 is a two-storey red brick building in traditional Southern Fujian style. Facing west, it measures 8.4m wide and 5.7m deep, covering about 82.3 square metres. The dado on the ground floor is made of granite, and the walls themselves are made of red bricks. The roof, in a gable style, is made of red planks and tiles, while the ridge is in a saddle style. The front door holds a plaque saying "Wangui Lianfang". (Photo by Zheng Shuizhong)

◎ 金门县政府文书房位于田垱北里 123 号和 124 号。123 号为西式两层洋楼，坐北朝南，面宽 8.4 米，进深 5.7 米，建筑面积约 95.7 平方米。建筑梁架为现浇钢筋水泥结构，楼面及屋面为木结构。124 号是闽南传统红砖建筑，坐东朝西，面宽 11.4 米，进深 11 米，建筑面积约 125 平方米。主体建筑屋顶为硬山顶，屋脊起翘呈燕尾式。（郑水忠 摄）

Jinmen County Government Secretariat Office is located at No.123 and No.124 Tianqian North Road. No. 123 is a Western-style two-storey building that faces south. It measures 8.4m wide, 5.7m deep, with a total floor space of 95.7 square metres. The frame of the building is cast in place concrete, and the floor and roof are made of wood. No. 124 is a red brick building in traditional Southern Fujian style, facing west. It measures 11.4m wide, 11m deep, with a floor space of 125 square metres. The building is set up with gabled roof and swallowtail ridge. (Photo by Zheng Shuizhong)

◎ 金门县政府会议旧址（郑氏家庙）是田墘村的中心建筑，在金门县政府内迁田墘村之后，主要作为金门县政府举行大会的会议场所。郑氏家庙坐东朝西，是大嶝红砖聚落的代表性建筑，为闽南传统宗祠类建筑，以红色为主色调，面宽 12 米，进深 23.7 米，占地面积 284.4 平方米。前殿石壁角雕有万字纹、团鹤、麒麟等图案。（杨振元 摄）

The former site of Jinmen County Government Conference (Zheng Family's Ancestral Hall) is the central building of Tianqian Village. After the relocation of the Jinmen County Government to Tianqian Village, this building was the primary conferencing place for the government. Zheng Family's Ancestral Hall faces west and is a characteristic red brick building and a traditional Southern Fujian ancestral hall. Primarily red in colour, it is 12m wide, 23.7m deep, with a floor space of 284.4 square metres. The stone wall at the front of the building is carved with the patterns of swastika(卍), cranes and kylin. (Photo by Yang Zhenyuan)

◎ 金门县政府保安队队址为田墘南里 415 号，位于郑氏祖祠南侧。建筑坐南朝北，为两层闽南传统红砖建筑。面宽 15 米，进深 4 米，建筑面积约 120 平方米。（郑水忠 摄）

The former site of Jinmen County Government Security Force Headquarters is located at No. 415 Tianqian South Road, south of Zheng Family's Ancestral Hall. The building faces north and is a two-storey red brick building in traditional Southern Fujian style. It is 15m wide, 4m deep, with a floor space of about 120 square metres. (Photo by Zheng Shuizhong)

◎ 国民党金门县党部书记处位于田墘南里 418 号，为闽南传统红砖建筑。建筑坐西朝东，建筑面积约 280 平方米。主体建筑面宽 15.2 米，进深 11.3 米，明间为厅，两侧为厢房。护厝为两层建筑，面宽 4.3 米，进深 11.3 米。外墙墙裙为花岗岩块石砌筑，主体建筑墙身为红砖铺砌，屋顶为硬山顶，屋脊起翘呈燕尾式。（杨振元 摄）

The Office of Kuomintang's Jinmen County Party Secretariat is located at No. 418 Tianqian South Road. Of traditional Southern Fujian red brick architectural style, it faces east, standing 15.2m wide, 11.3m deep, with a floor space of about 280 square metres. There is a main hall and two wing rooms. There is also a two-storey guardhouse that is 4.3m wide and 11.3m deep. The dado of the outer wall is of granite, and the wall itself is of red brick. The building is of gabled roof and swallowtail ridge. (Photo by Yang Zhenyuan)

◎ 金门县政府盐兵楼为两层西式洋楼，坐北朝南，面宽 8.4 米，进深 5.7 米，建筑面积约 95.7 平方米。盐兵楼的灰白檐顶侧边是西式风格，红砖廊柱又使其充满中国色彩。房檐贴有白底红花绿叶瓷砖，全部是从日本购得，至今色彩鲜艳。楼顶石雕则是中国传统菊花造型与西式飞兽相融合。二楼前廊为红砖砌筑，立面由欧式拱形柱廊组成。（郑水忠 摄）

The Jinmen County Government Defensive Fort is a Western-style two-storey building. It faces south, standing 8.4m wide, 5.7m deep with a floor space of about 95.7 square metres. The top ridge on the roof is of a Western style, yet the vibrant red brick colonnades of the building make it undoubtedly Chinese. The eaves are decorated with ceramic tiles of red flowers and green leaves on a white background, which were imported from Japan. There are traditional Chinese stone carvings of chrysanthemums, as well as Western style gargoyles on the top floor. The façade is of red brick on the second-floor balcony and elsewhere, in the style of European arched colonnades. (Photo by Zheng Shuizhong)

◎ 国民党金门县党部楼群位于田墩南里 337 号、351 号和 355
号。337 号、355 号建筑为闽南传统红砖建筑，351 号建筑
为中西合璧两层洋楼。337 号建筑坐东朝西，面宽 11.4 米，
进深 21 米，建筑面积约 239.4 平方米。前落面阔 3 间，进
深 1 间，明间为门厅，两侧为厢房。355 号建筑坐东朝西，
面宽 15.1 米，进深 21.7 米，建筑面积约 328.3 平方米。前
落面阔 3 间，进深 1 间，明间为门厅，两侧为厢房。351 号
为规模宏大的中西合璧两层洋楼，并附有一列平屋。主楼坐
北朝南，面宽 11.4 米，进深 12.9 米，建筑面积 294 平方米。
351 号建筑主体为砖混结构，楼面为木结构。平屋坐南朝北，
与主楼相对，两侧以围墙合围成一闭合体。平屋面宽 11.4 米，
进深 4.5 米，建筑面积约 51 平方米，砖木结构。（郑水忠 摄）

The Kuomintang's Jinmen County Party Office are located at Nos.
337, 351, 355 of Tianqian South Road. Nos. 337 and 355 are red
brick buildings in traditional Southern Fujian style, and No. 351
is a two-storey building combining both Chinese and Western
architectural styles. No. 337 faces west, measuring 11.4m wide,
21m deep, covering an area of about 239.4 square metres. The
first courtyard is three rooms wide and one room deep. Entering
the courtyard, you will face the main hall, with wing rooms on
both sides. No. 355 also faces west, measuring 15.1m wide, 21.7m
deep, with a floor space of about 328.3 square metres. It is similar
to the building of No. 337 in terms of courtyard layout, with the
same main hall and wing rooms. The first courtyard is three rooms
wide and one room deep too. No. 351 is a large two-storey
building that combines Chinese and Western styles and affiliated
with a row of one-storey buildings. The main building faces south,
measuring 11.4m wide, 12.9m deep and boasts a total floor space
of 294 square metres. The body of building No. 351 is a mix of
concrete and brick, and the façade is of wood. The one-storey
building faces north, just opposite the main building. The two sets
of buildings are joined by walls on both sides, creating a courtyard
in the middle. The one-storey building are 11.4m wide, 4.5m deep,
with a total floor space of about 51 square metres, made of brick
and wood. (Photo by Zheng Shuizhong)

万里茶道（中国福建段）
The Ten-Thousand-Li Tea Road (Fujian Section in China)

通往欧洲各国

中俄贸易城
恰克图

（现乌兰巴托

归北（现呼和浩特）
张家口
县
太原
祁县
长治
洛阳
旗镇
唐河
襄樊
汉口
江西河口
（现铅山县）
武夷山下梅　（福州
潮州
香港

© 万里茶道起点——中国福建武夷山下梅村（郑友裕 摄）
The start of the Ten-Thousand-Li Tea Road——Xiamei Village, Wuyishan, Fujian, China. (Photo by Zheng Youyu)

遗产价值

万里茶道是 17 世纪末至 20 世纪初古代中国与俄国之间以茶叶为大宗贸易商品的长距离商业贸易路线，也是继古代丝绸之路衰落之后在亚欧大陆兴起的又一条重要的国际商道。该线路南起福建武夷山等中国南方的山地产茶区，所运茶叶经水陆交替运输北上，经汉口、张家口集散转运，沿途经过福建、江西、湖北、湖南、河南、山西、河北、内蒙古八省（区），过蒙古国库伦（乌兰巴托的旧称）后一直运至古代中俄边境茶叶通商口岸城市恰克图，在此完成交易后辗转销往西伯利亚、莫斯科、圣彼得堡和欧洲，干线总长 14,000 余公里。该线路沟通了亚洲大陆南北方向农耕文明与草原游牧文明的核心区域，并延伸至中亚和东欧等地区，展现了茶叶成为全球性商品的世界性贸易盛期。

◎ 当年恰克图茶市的盛况。（文脉 供图）
A grand occasion of the tea market in Kyakhta at that time. (Courtesy of Wenmai)

◎ 恰克图茶商合作社的广告。（文脉 供图）

A leaflet advertising the tea merchants' cooperative in Kyakhta. (Courtesy of Wenmai)

Universal Value

The Ten-Thousand-*Li* Tea Road was a commercial trade route running between ancient China and Russia from the late 17th century to the beginning of the 20th century, the primary commodity being tea. It was an important international trade route that emerged in Eurasia after the decline of the ancient Silk Road. Starting from Fujian's Mount Wuyi and other mountainous tea producing areas in southern China, the tea was transported north across both land and sea to Hankou and Zhangjiakou, from where it was further distributed. To reach its destination, the tea travelled through Fujian, Jiangxi, Hubei, Hunan, Henan, Shanxi, Hebei, and Inner Mongolia. After making it to Kulun (now Ulaanbaatar) in Mongolia, the trade route crossed the Sino-Russian border at Kyakhta, a small trading village, which then connected to Siberia, Moscow, St. Petersburg and farther west towards Europe, resulting in a trade route that stretched over 14,000 kilometres. The route connected key areas of the agricultural and nomadic civilizations from north to south across the Asian continent, and extended west towards Central Asia and Eastern Europe, giving rise to the prosperous worldwide tea trade.

◎ 位于武夷山下梅村的邹氏家祠造型精美，气势恢宏，体现了当时茶商的经济实力。（郑友裕 摄）

Located in Xiamei Village at the foot of Mount Wuyi, the magnificent Zou Family Ancestral Hall is elaborately decorated, a reflection of the wealth of tea merchants during this time. (Photo by Zheng Youyu)

　　万里茶道（中国段）沿线的城市、集镇、村落、建筑及交通体系，在 17 世纪末至 20 世纪初因跨区域茶叶贸易的繁荣而产生了类型、功能、格局、形式等方面的发展，展现出传统农业文明社会受到近代商业文明发展的明显影响，以及茶路沿线多个地理文化区域间的观念、文化、技术交流。

　　由茶园、工厂、古道、码头、集镇、会馆、海关、银行、寺庙、宅院等遗存构成的系列遗产整体，则体现了茶叶贸易所涉及的生产、加工、运输、销售及相关文化生活的完整环节，共同见证了这一时期长距离、跨区域的中俄茶叶商贸体系、运行模式和商人群体的生活方式。

The tea trade contributed greatly to the development of cities, markets, villages, and architectural and transportation systems along the Ten-Thousand-*Li* Tea Road. During the time, the previously traditional agricultural societies were significantly affected by this modern commercial phenomenon, which facilitated the exchange of ideas, culture and technology between the various societies along the trade route.

Cultural heritage sites that remain from the tea trade include tea estates, factories, ancient roads, wharves, trading posts, guild halls, customs offices, banks, temples, private houses and so on, a result of the complex journey that involved the production, processing, transportation and sale of tea, as well as the relevant culture. Together, these individual pieces bore witness to an elaborate long distance inter-regional and international tea trade, its system and modes of operation, and the merchants' lifestyle change associated with it.

◎ 武夷山下梅村天一井是清代茶商用来取水斗茶的井。（郑友裕 摄）

Tianyi Well in Xiamei Village at the foot of Mount Wuyi was a source of water for tea competitions popular among the Qing Dynasty tea merchants. (Photo by Zheng Youyu)

在南北向超万公里的长距离茶叶运输和贸易中，沿线的工厂、古道、码头、关隘、城镇的建设或利用，水、陆转运体系及马、车、船、驼结合的运输方式，呈现出在当时传统交通方式条件下，对中国由南向北的丘陵山地、水网平原、山间盆地、高原等复杂多变地形及环境的杰出应对。

这条国际商路与世界性的产茶、茶饮生活传统，与东南亚范围内共有的关公信仰，与作为古代中国金融组织代表性产物的票号均有直接的关联。

◎ 坐落于"大清金融第一街"平遥古城西大街的日昇昌票号，现为中国票号博物馆。（壹图网 供图）
Rishengchang Piaohao (a dradft bank), now a Piaohao museum, situated at the so-called "First Financial Avenue of the Qing Dynasty" in the West Street of the Ancient City of Ping Yao, Shanxi. (Courtesy of www.1tu.com)

◎ 1880 年英国商人在中国福州茶叶品尝室中品茶的场景。（文脉 供图）

A scene of English merchants drinking tea at a tasting room in Fuzhou, China in 1880. (Courtesy of Wenmai)

The tea trade stretched over 14,000 kilometres, necessitating the construction of factories, ancient roads, shipping piers, passes and trading posts, as well as improved use of land and sea based on trade routes, and complex transportation methods utilising horses, carts, ships and camels, exemplifying the ingenuity of ancient China's response to the various complex terrains and environments that needed to be traversed, including hills, mountains, waters, plains, valleys and plateaus.

This international trade route is directly related to worldwide tea producing and tea drinking traditions, the prevalence of belief in Sir Guangong in Southeast Asia, and the existence of Piaohao (draft banks), a representative of financial organizations in ancient China.

© 茶事题刻所在地——武夷山九曲溪。（郑友裕 摄）

The cliff inscriptions about tea affairs can be found along Nine-Bend Stream. (Photo by Zheng Youyu)

福建武夷山，是这条古老茶道的起点——茶叶从武夷山及周边产区运至武夷山下梅村、赤石村、星村等大型集散地，船从下梅经当溪、梅溪入崇阳溪，过星村，抵达崇安县城城关，沿闽赣古驿道走陆路，经分水关等闽赣界关进入江西境内，一路北上。武夷茶产区、九曲溪茶事题刻、下梅传统村落、闽赣古驿道及分水关遗址成为岁月在这条漫漫长路上为武夷山留下的 4 处最具代表性的史迹遗址（聚落）。

Mount Wuyi in Fujian is the starting point of this ancient trade route. The tea produced in the area was transported to larger distribution centres such as Xiamei Village, Chishi Village, Xingcun Village, then via boat from Dangxi Creek and Meixi Creek in Xiamei to Chongyang Creek before arriving at Chongan County. It was then transported by land to cross the Fujian-Jiangxi border, and then northward. The Tea Planting and Processing Area in Mount Wuyi, the Cliff Inscriptions about Tea Affairs along Nine-Bend Stream, the Traditional Xiamei Village, the Fujian-Jiangxi Ancient Roads and Fenshuiguan Historic Site are four exemplary historic remnants left behind in Mount Wuyi along this long tea road.

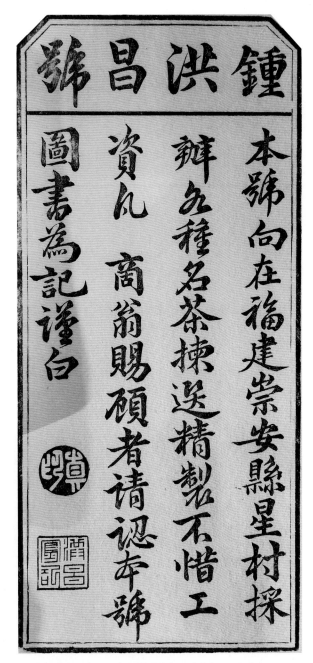

◎ 当时的茶叶商号习惯于将采购自福建崇安县（今武夷山地区）星村作为卖点宣传。（文脉 供图）

Tea shops at that time used to advertise their tea by telling customers that it was booked from Xingcun Village, Chongan County (now the Mount Wuyi area), Fujian. (Courtesy of Wenmai)

茶道起点访古

■ 武夷茶产区

　　据《崇安县新志》（1940年）记载："武夷茶，始于唐，盛于宋元，衰于明，而复兴于清。"武夷山及其周边地区自唐宋以来就是茶产地，明清两代已蜚声世界，构成了万里茶道大批量茶、高端茶的核心生产区域。武夷山大坑口古茶园、蓑衣岭古茶园、马头岩古茶园、喊山台古茶园以及佛国岩茶厂遗址均见证了当时茶事的兴盛。

◎ 大坑口古茶园海拔198米，总面阔148米，总进深62米，由北向南依山势而建，呈阶梯式，以种植肉桂为主，挡土护坡用丹霞石垒砌。（吴心正 摄）

Dakengkou Ancient Tea Estate is 198m above sea level, stretching 148m wide and 62m deep. Built into the mountain, there are very clear terraces distributed from north to south. Primarily a source of Rougui (Cinnamon), the terraces are built with Danxia stones to prevent loss of soil. (Photo by Wu Xinzheng)

◎ 大坑口古茶园一隅。（郑友裕 摄）

A corner of Dakengkou Ancient Tea Estate. (Photo by Zheng Youyu)

◎ 蓑衣岭古茶园海拔 380 米，斜长 202 米，宽 5.8—30 米，为大体呈南北走向的长条形梯式茶园，梯田沿山间小路两侧分布，茶树依蓑衣岭岩壁而植。（吴心正 摄）

Suoyiling Tea Estate is at an altitude of 380m, with a slanting length of 202m and width ranging from 5.8m to 30m. It is a long and narrow terraced tea plantation, running north to south. A small path runs through the middle; tea terraces flourish on either side, and tea trees are planted along Suoyiling rock walls. (Photo by Wu Xinzheng)

Remains at the Starting Point of the Tea Road

■ Tea Planting and Processing Area in Mount Wuyi

According to *The New Records of Chongan County* (1940), Wuyi Tea was first produced during the Tang Dynasty, flourished during the Song and Yuan dynasties, declined during the Ming Dynasty and revived during the Qing Dynasty. Having been tea producing areas since the Tang Dynasty, Mount Wuyi and its surrounding areas became world-famous during the Ming and Qing dynasties. As core production areas, they produced tea in large quantities and of high-quality that was shipped on the Ten-Thousand-*Li* Tea Road. The ancient tea terraces of Dakengkou, Suoyiling, Matouyan, Hanshantai and the site of Foguoyan Tea Factory are testaments to the prosperity of the tea trade.

◎ 马头岩古茶园海拔约 380 米，总面积约 102 亩，主要分布在马头岩岩下，大体呈半圆形阶梯状，以种植肉桂为主。（吴心正 摄）

Matouyan Ancient Tea Estate is at an altitude of about 380m, covering an area of approximately 16.8 acres. It is located at the foot of Matouyan (Horse Head Rock). The terraces are arranged in a semi-circular fashion, and the most common variety of tea is Rougui (Cinnamon). (Photo by Wu Xinzheng)

◎ 喊山台古茶园主要分布在喊山台山谷之间、山间小路两侧，为大体呈东西走向的长条形梯式茶园，茶树依岩壁而植，主要品种为大红袍、肉桂、铁罗汉等。喊山是一种古老的祭祀风俗，旨在祈求神灵保佑茶叶丰收、茶事顺利。（吴心正 摄）

Hanshantai Ancient Tea Estate is found in the valleys of Hanshantai, composed of a series of east-west running strips on either side of the mountain path. The main varieties grown here include Dahongpao (Big Red Robe), Rougui (Cinnamon) and Tieluohan (Iron Arhat). "Hanshan", literally translated to yelling into the mountains, is an ancient tradition that acts as a prayer for the gods to bless the tea harvest and ensure success for the tea trade. (Photo by Wu Xinzheng)

◎ 佛国岩茶厂遗址的原有木构建筑已毁，仅存墙基、柱础、天井，现地面建筑为 20 世纪建造。厂区南侧为作坊区，北侧为居住区。（吴心正 摄）

The original wooden structure at the site of Foguoyan Tea Factory was destroyed long ago, and only parts of the foundation survive. The current factory was constructed in the 20th century, with a workshop in the southern part and the residential area in its north. (Photo by Wu Xinzheng)

■ 九曲溪茶事题刻

　　茶事的兴盛还体现在武夷山景区九曲溪两岸的石壁上所保存的五方摩崖石刻，分别为明万历四十三年（1615）建宁府衙题刻、清康熙三十五年（1696）福建按察使司告示、清康熙三十五年（1696）崇安县衙告示、清康熙五十三年（1714）福建陆路提督告示、清乾隆二十八年（1763）建宁府告示。主要内容是保护当地茶农、茶僧利益，打击假借官府名义行勒索之事的衙役和小吏，镌刻在摩崖石壁上，以达到警示目的。这些题刻反映了当时地方政府关于茶政的地方治理和乡村控制，是万里茶道文化遗产重要而特殊的组成部分，也是明清时期地方政府保护茶叶产业发展的记忆遗产。

◎ 明万历四十三年建宁府衙题刻，内容包含减免茶税、禁止强买勒索等，是武夷山现存摩崖石刻中最早的保护茶农利益的官府布告。（吴心正 摄）

The inscription of the 1615 Decree issued by the then Jianning Government. The contents include reductions and exemptions for tea producers, prohibition of extortion and other laws. It was the first official announcement issued to protect tea farmers found among Mount Wuyi's extant cliff inscriptions. (Photo by Wu Xinzheng)

■ The Cliff Inscriptions about Tea Affairs along Nine-Bend Stream

The opulence of the tea trade can be seen from five cliff inscriptions on either side of Nine-Bend Stream in Wuyishan scenic area. Each inscription is different. The first was inscribed in 1615, commissioned by the Jianning Government at the time. In 1696, two inscriptions were made, one an announcement by the provincial judicial official, and the other an announcement by the Chongan County government. In 1714, another announcement was made by the top provincial military officer, and the Jianning Government commissioned the fifth one in 1763. Inscribed on the cliff as a warning, these announcements were made to protect the interests of local tea farmers and monks and avoid corrupt government officials misusing their power to threaten ordinary tea producers. A reflection of past governmental system to manage and protect the tea industry, these inscriptions are a special cultural legacy from the Ming and Qing dynasties on the tea road.

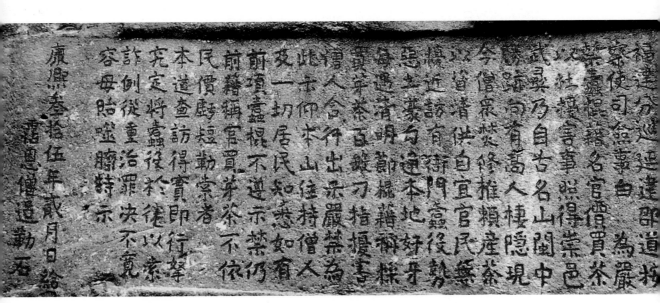

◎ 清康熙三十五年福建按察使司告示，称对不依民价、亏短勒索者"即行拿究""决不宽容"。（郑友裕 摄）

The 1696 Announcement by the provincial judicial official that outlines a zero-tolerance policy for driving down purchasing price, shortchanging and extorting tea farmers. (Photo by Zheng Youyu)

◎ 下梅大夫第是万里茶道第一代开拓人之一邹英章为庆祝自己的六十大寿而建。（翁培义 摄）
Xiamei Dafu Mansion was built by Zou Yingzhang, one of the first generation of tea road pioneers, to celebrate his 60th birthday.
(Photo by Weng Peiyi)

■ 下梅传统村落

　　下梅村地处武夷山梅溪下游，清初，在以常氏为代表的晋商和以下梅邹氏为代表的武夷山本土商帮的携手推动下，这里逐渐成为万里茶道上的大宗茶叶集散地，风靡欧洲的武夷茶由此开启北上旅程。今日的下梅村依旧群山环抱、溪水叮咚，以清初开凿的人工运河当溪为轴，两侧保存了古民居、码头、古井、古桥、古街等，使之尽享中国历史文化名村、中国传统村落、万里茶道文化线路标志性核心节点村镇等美誉。现存的与茶叶贸易相关的主要文物建筑包括当溪及埠头、邹氏家祠、下梅大夫第、下梅西水别业、景隆号茶庄、天一井、镇国庙等，以及可移动文物——"民巘轩"牌匾。

■ The Traditional Xiamei Village

Xiamei Village is downstream of Meixi Stream in the Mount Wuyi area. In the early Qing Dynasty, merchants from Shanxi, represented by the Chang family, and local merchants in Mount Wuyi, represented by the Zou family, decided to work together, making Xiamei Village an important distribution centre for tea. It was from here that the journey of Wuyi Tea, which was then very popular in Europe, began. Today, Xiamei Village is idyllic, surrounded by green mountains and tinkling rivers. Dangxi Stream, an artificial canal dug during the early Qing Dynasty, serves as the central axis and provides an excellent water source; and the ancient dwellings, wharves, wells, bridges and streets around it are still very well preserved, making Xiamei one of China's famous traditional villages and a key landmark on the Ten-Thousand-Li Tea Road. Still extant cultural heritage includes Dangxi Stream and Wharf, the Zou Family Ancestral Hall, Xiamei Dafu Mansion, Xiamei Xishui Villa, Jinglonghao Teahouse, Tianyi Well, Zhenguo Temple and the portable artifact "Minyixuan Plaque".

◎ "民艤轩" 牌匾。（郑友裕 摄）
"Minyixuan" Plaque. (Photo by Zheng Youyu)

■ 闽赣古驿道及分水关遗址

　　福建多山，古时交通不便，闽赣古驿道是新石器时代以来福建先民与中原交流的重要通道，商旅往来、军事攻防、八闽学子进京赶考、各级官员晋京，大多由此通行。它充分利用两省交界区域山形地貌，经过历代官方和民间共同经营而成，以两省交界的关隘为主要标志。万里茶道的许多路段也是依托历史形成的古驿道，其中崇安县城城关至闽赣交界分水关段就属于此类型。分水关的具体建成年代尚需考证，至迟在唐代已经存在。

◎ 分水关古驿道。（翁培义 摄）
Fenshuiguan Ancient Road. (Photo by Weng Peiyi)

◎ 分水关古驿道碑遗址。（翁培义 摄）

The site of the Stone Tablet of Fenshuiguan Ancient Road. (Photo by Weng Peiyi)

■ The Fujian-Jiangxi Ancient Roads and Fenshuiguan Historic Site

Fujian is a mountainous province, making transportation a difficult task in ancient times. The ancient roads between Fujian and Jiangxi were incredibly important, allowing for communication between Fujian and the Central Plains since the Neolithic Age. They also served to transport military, facilitate trade, and make it possible for Fujian examinees and officials to visit the capital. Using the pass as a landmark, the road made great use of the mountainous terrain bordering the two provinces and was operated by both the civil and official force over ages. Many sections of the Ten-Thousand-*Li* Tea Road were also ancient roads formed under similar historical conditions, and the section from the area of Chongan County to the province border of Fujian-Jiangxi, namely Fenshuiguan, was one of them. The exact construction date of Fenshuiguan is unknown, but it has existed since at least the Tang Dynasty.

◎ 大安岭段驿道整体保存基本完整，陡峭处间隔1—1.2米左右铺设长条形石阶，石阶西端有榫卯，专家推测这些榫卯是用来安装护栏的，以便挑夫休息。（翁培义 摄）

The road section at Da'anling is practically intact. The roadbed where it is steep was paved with rectangle slates with intervals of 1—1.2m, and on the west side are mortises in the stones, which experts believe to have held wooden posts in the past for porters to rest themselves. (Photo by Weng Peiyi)

　　从下梅沿崇阳溪北上的茶叶，在崇安改行陆地，翻越分水关，进入江西铅山河口码头后再次上船。据《崇安县新志》记载，当时崇安至江西铅山一带，"车马之声，昼夜不息"。古驿道现存有大安岭段驿道、黄莲坑段驿道、中蓬段驿道、苏州馆驿道、大安岭井、黄莲坑卷桥、孤魂总祭碑与祠、分水关遗址等。上述驿道大体呈东南—西北走向，由长方形条石、大小不一的河卵石铺设而成。

The tea that left Xiamei Village following Chongyang Stream was transferred to land-based trade routes, passing Fenshuiguan before arriving in Jiangxi, where it was once again loaded onto ships at Hekou Wharf in Yanshan. According to *The New Records of Chongan County*, the entire stretch from Chongan to Yanshan was filled with "the sounds of horses and carriages, continuous even through the night". Several roads that formed part of the trade route are extant, including sections at Da'anling, Huangliankeng, Zhongpeng, and Suzhouguan. Other historic sites that lie along the roads are Da'anling Well, Huangliankeng Juanqiao Bridge, Guhun Memorial Tablet and Hall, and Fenshuiguan. Most of these roads went southeast to northwest, paved with rectangle slates and cobblestones of varying sizes.

◎ 黄莲坑卷桥。（翁培义 摄）
Huangliankeng Juanqiao Bridge. (Photo by Weng Peiyi)

◎ 孤魂总祭碑与祠。祭碑立于清光绪六年（1880）春月，祭祀的是茶道上来自江西、安徽等省份的那些依靠给过往客商搬运货物为生计却客死他乡的外省人。（翁培义 摄）

Guhun Memorial Tablet and Hall. The tablet was erected in 1880 to commemorate outlanders from other provinces like Jiangxi and Anhui, who made a living by carrying goods (mainly tea) for passing merchants but unfortunately died on the tea road. (Photo by Weng Peiyi)

《福建的文化与自然遗产》编写组

主　编：傅柒生

副主编：何经平

中　文：宋　春　余亿明　林　叶　苏　西　常　浩

　　　　田成海　李熙慧

英　文：Richard Howe　Donna Jiang　Rocky Jiang

　　　　Cassidy Gong　陈小慰　池　玫　陈钰茜

　　　　黄兆儒　谢旻怡

图书在版编目（CIP）数据

福建的文化与自然遗产：汉英对照 / 福建省人民政府
新闻办公室编 . --福州：福建人民出版社，2021.7
ISBN 978-7-211-08521-7

Ⅰ.①福… Ⅱ.①福… Ⅲ.①文化遗产—介绍—福建—
汉、英 Ⅳ.①K295.7

中国版本图书馆 CIP 数据核字（2020）第 187833 号

福建的文化与自然遗产
FUJIAN DE WENHUA YU ZIRAN YICHAN

中　　文：宋　春　余亿明　林　叶　苏　西　常　浩　田成海　李熙慧
英　　文：Richard Howe　　Donna Jiang　　Rocky Jiang　　Cassidy Gong
　　　　　陈小慰　池　玫　陈钰茜　黄兆儒　谢旻怡
责任编辑：周跃进　李文淑　孙　颖
美术编辑：白　玫
内文排版：雅昌文化（集团）有限公司
出版发行：福建人民出版社　　　　　　　电　　话：0591-87533169(发行部)
网　　址：http://www.fjpph.com　　　　电子邮箱：fjpph7211@126.com
地　　址：福州市东水路 76 号　　　　　邮政编码：350001
经　　销：福建新华发行（集团）有限责任公司
印　　刷：雅昌文化（集团）有限公司
地　　址：深圳市南山区深云路 19 号
开　　本：787 毫米×1092 毫米　　1/16
印　　张：18.75
字　　数：546 千字
版　　次：2021 年 7 月第 1 版
印　　次：2021 年 7 月第 1 次印刷
书　　号：ISBN 978-7-211-08521-7
定　　价：198.00 元